The REACTION Dashboard

# The REACTION Dashboard:

The simple tool leaders use to understand, assess, and improve organizational culture.

By Chris Wignall
www.catalystfoundation.ca

*The REACTION Dashboard Copyright © 2018 by Chris Wignall. All Rights Reserved.*

*Deep thanks to all the leaders who have allowed me to be a part of their stories. You have taught me far more than I have taught you.*

*Thank you Shirley and Doug for taking repeated risks with me as we've shared this wonderful experiment we call Catalyst Foundation, and particularly this often delayed writing project.*

*My mom infused me with the power of stories, a desire to teach, and demonstrated the value of giving yourself for the benefit of others.*

*Ben, Ian, and Amy: You are my biggest motivations for helping leaders. I want you to follow great leaders and become people who change the world without losing your selves and your souls in the process.*

*Kristen: Thank you for indulging my distraction in this project; all the delays, frustrations, and time it took to get this thing done. I love you.*

Philippians 3:10-12

# Contents

| | |
|---|---|
| Endorsements | ix |
| Foreword | xiii |
| Introduction | 1 |
| | |
| The Story | 5 |
| Chapter One - An Uncertain Beginning | 6 |
| The REACTION Dashboard | 12 |
| Chapter Two - Celebration?!? | 13 |
| Chapter Three - Reason | 18 |
| Chapter Four - Energy | 23 |
| Chapter Five - Alignment | 29 |
| Chapter Six - Clarity | 34 |
| Chapter Seven - Trust | 39 |
| Chapter Eight - Epilogue | 45 |
| The Elements | 51 |
| The Elements - Reason | 52 |
| The Elements - Energy | 61 |
| The Elements - Alignment | 70 |
| The Elements - Clarity | 76 |
| The Elements - Trust | 83 |
| The Elements - Celebration | 90 |
| User's Guide to The REACTION Dashboard | 96 |
| The REACTION Dashboard Worksheet | 105 |
| A Final Word | 106 |

# About The Author

# Endorsements

"Creating an optimized Organizational Culture is a key priority for most CEO's. The REACTION Dashboard provides both a compelling rationale to improve your Organizations' Culture and the pragmatic process and tools you will need to be successful! "
-Sue Wigston, Chief Operating Officer, Eagle's Flight

"Another book on leadership?? Really?? Am I ever glad I read this one! Chris Wignall provides us with an engaging, eminently readable and understandable book that provides straightforward and sensible solutions to many of the complex challenges faced by leaders both individually and organizationally. Wignall's considerable experience working with leaders and his engaging narrative style quickly overcame any skepticism on my part. As I read, I found myself processing my own leadership challenges and began using the dashboard to assess how I was doing as a leader and how we were doing as an organization. I loved the chapter on celebration! Like Wignall, I have a stack of leadership books lining my shelves. The REACTION Dashboard is the shortest and amongst the most practical and enjoyable I have read in a very long time."
– Peter Roebbelen, President, The Charis Foundation, and Author of *Mercy: Life in the Season of Dying*

"Unlike leadership concepts such as strategic planning or goal-setting, building a healthy culture has long been considered essential, but somehow elusive. Largely this is because culture seems so hard to define, let alone assess and improve. But with The REACTION Dashboard, Chris Wignall has come up with tool that with help you do just that. The book is easy to read, but don't let that fool you. It contains powerful truths that can be applied to make an immediate impact on the health of your team's culture."

-Scott Cochrane, Vice President International Ministries, Willow Creek Association

"The REACTION Dashboard is an excellent primer for executives in the public/private & charitable sectors to assess and improve the most important element of any organization, its culture. I highly recommend this book by Chris Wignall."
-Terry Cooke, President & CEO, Hamilton Community Foundation

"Chris Wignall has given us a true gift here, *The REACTION Dashboard* is more than just another title in the stack of books on organizational culture, it's a helpful tool that energizes organizational possibilities and cultures."
−Christopher L. Heuertz, Founding Partner of Gravity, a Center for Contemplative Activism and Author of *The Sacred Enneagram: Finding Your Unique Path to Spiritual Growth.*

"For many years, the consultant Lyle Schaller was the master of tucking lessons inside stories. It's the skill of a journalist combined with that of an imaginative teacher. Being carried along by the wisdom that comes across so naturally and finding creative ways to provide tools for genuine learning makes The REACTION Dashboard a successor to Lyle Schaller's unique style and content."
-Fred Smith Jr., President, The Gathering

"In today's increasingly competitive, fast paced and constant change environment, leading a complex organization has never been harder. It also means there is a greater need for leaders to create a culture where our people are both challenged and cared for in the midst of competing demands for time and energy. Chris's REACTION Dashboard is refreshingly simple, practical, and memorable. It's a leadership book that you'll actually use. The emphasis on the power of Celebration alone has the potential to make many leaders and organizations healthier and more impactful. This books is well worth the read particularly for those leaders looking to better focus their energy and time to drive positive results and culture."

-Caroline Riseboro, President and CEO, PLAN International Canada
"Simply put, The Reaction Dashboard is a rare find. It will help you, your team and your organization purposefully reflect, effectively evaluate, and practically move toward greater health and impact. It's a leadership tool that's easy to grasp, simple to use and refreshingly actionable."
-Dr. Steve Brown, President, Arrow Leadership and author of *Leading Me – Eight Practices for a Christian Leader's Most Important Assignment*
"On hiking trails you'll see dangerously under-equipped and horrendously over-equipped trekkers, each equally set up for trouble. Then along comes a hiking aficionado whose compact pack contains just the essentials, precisely selected and artfully arranged. This is what Chris' book is for leaders. He has provided us with a clear and concise set of tools, useful on any leadership trail, and with just the right amount of explanation for immediate application. At the same time, Chris provides a bit of his own trail wisdom, just enough to help the reader along. Eminently practical but life-giving basics for any leadership situation: get it."
-Jonathan Wilson, President & CEO, Soul Systems
"Wow! What a gift! The REACTION Dashboard is a fantastic tool for your organization to move towards a deeper sense of true effectiveness. Get a stack of these books for your team and apply these lessons to the mission you're called to!"
-Rich Birch, UnSeminary, Author of *Unreasonable Churches* and *The Church Growth Flywheel*
"This is a wonderful book and a fantastic tool. I couldn't agree more that in order to truly impact culture, first you have to understand an organization's reason to exist. From there, you build your culture, remembering to celebrate along the way!"
-Janet Noel-Annable, CEO, Christian Horizons
"I would encourage anyone who cares about the health of their organization to give Chris' REACTION dashboard a try. As an organizational health fanatic – with experience to back it up – Chris' passion oozes from the pages of this book. Hear his heart,

get into his head and implement his model to make your organization better!"

-Jeff Lockyer, Lead Pastor, Southridge Community Church

"There are times when a leader just needs someone to sit down with them, and draw a simple diagram on a napkin. This is exactly what Chris Wignall has done for us in sharing this clarifying tool. You will find the ability to focus both you and your team in the simplicity of the approach. I recommend this as a tool we should be teaching to every leader we work with."

-Dr. Carson Pue, Executive Mentor | Author | Speaker, Author of *Mentoring Leaders*

# Foreword

Culture is a buzzword for every leader these days. Culture is usually associated with what people often call "the soft stuff" – how people feel, their attitudes, how trusting they are, how openly they communicate... If you haven't figured out that this "soft stuff" is the hardest stuff to work on, you haven't yet felt the true weight of leadership.

I've spent the past 25 years helping leaders improve their organizations – at the board level and in the C-suite. My colleagues and I quickly concluded that as important as "smart" is (and this refers to the more concrete aspects of business like strategy and financing and technology and compensation), "healthy" (doing well on the soft stuff) is where the real opportunities for breakthrough lie. Chris Wignall has been a provocative fellow soldier in this battle and we've enjoyed many long talks comparing struggles, sharing advances, and attempting to clarify patterns of traction in the journey. Any time we found a tool that helped or an approach that worked, we'd be eager to offer them to each other. So I've had the benefit of seeing the REACTION Dashboard proposed and tested and refined over years. I'm so glad that this framework – this well-used tool – is now being shared with the broader world. We will all benefit from the experience and wisdom that Chris has accumulated.

Shaping culture is one of the most intangible responsibilities of a leader. We eventually internalize how important this is, but we never know how to quantify the payoff of investing our leadership horsepower to work on it. Some of us, however, have experienced the inescapable realization that taking our eye off that dimension of our business – usually because it was all going well and we hoped we were done with that – is costly indeed. Meetings that used to go smoothly and produce clarity now drag and end with lack of commitment. A vibe of "all for one and one for all" has been replaced by hallway complaints and resistance. As leader, you either direct your energy back to repairing this or you ignore it with the misguided hope that you can focus on results and drag everyone with you. Regardless, the tax of poor culture hits your financials eventually. You might not be able to calculate the precise amount, but you can't miss the substantial cost.

Chris has handed us a tool – literally a dashboard we can look at that show crucial information like the dashboards of our cars – to keep our eyes on indicators regarding culture. This will be revolutionary for most leaders because it finally tells us what to watch rather than be overwhelmed by the intangible nature of culture. Peppered throughout this helpful story are substantial nuggets drawn from over a decade of coaching leaders. You'll love Chris's attention to Celebration and you'll want to immediately come up with "a slogan, a story, a statistic, a symbol, and a strategy" to communicate your cause. The practical ideas and insights for improving culture are overflowing. For example, chapter 4 presents an actionable mix of approaches to help our people manage and recharge their energy for work. Chapter 7 is chock full of ways to work on trust in your organization. The back half of the book goes into much more detail about each of the elements of REACTION.

I earnestly hope you will take advantage of The REACTION Dashboard. It will inform your efforts to improve your organization. And when you are revelling in the progress, know that I will be part of the Network celebrating your success!

Jim Brown, Fall 2018

## Introduction

Like most leaders I have dozens, if not hundreds, of leadership books. They're on my shelves, beside my bed, in the back of my car, and in stacks throughout my home and office. Most of them have some good content; many are well written; a select few have become important to me because they brought a timely insight, a personal breakthrough, or a perspective I keep coming back to again and again.

You'll find this book is a little different. There's not a wealth of shiny new brilliance to be found on these pages. Most of what you'll read is probably what you already know through past learning or basic intuition. What you'll discover in The REACTION Dashboard is a simple, memorable, and extremely actionable tool to help you do what you already know is important: build a healthy culture.

The topic of organizational culture has gained a lot of traction in recent years. It's a much-needed companion to generations of good content on strategy and execution.

Most of us are well versed in at least the basics of strategy. We've had SMART goals drilled into us, and five-year plans (or hundred-year plans) are very familiar. There's really no excuse for any leader to not access solid strategy.

Similarly, we've trained in efficiency and productivity techniques. We know countless ways to set priorities and to make the most of our time and effort. Some of us struggle with the follow-through (raising my hand...), but we aren't lacking options.

Culture, on the other hand, has remained murky. Apart from academic pieces that are too complex for most leaders to apply, or simplistic slogans that are little more than clichés, most leaders are left without practical tools. We know at some level that culture is important, but we aren't clear on how to understand, assess, or improve it.

That's where The REACTION Dashboard comes in. This book is meant to help.

The REACTION Dashboard puts handles on the fuzzy concepts of culture, equipping us to take a good look at it and to identify risks and potential problems sooner, before they do serious damage. It enables leaders and teams to do a quick culture assessment as often as they want, at no financial cost, and in almost no time, with specific, practical, action steps every time.

Beyond that, The REACTION Dashboard elevates the importance of Celebration, an under-utilized practice that has huge leverage potential. Leaders and organizations who embrace the power of celebrating progress and impact can tap into levels of engagement that others just can't. The outcomes are remarkable.

How to read this book

The book is divided into three sections, to make it easy to find the parts that are most useful for each leader. I've laid it out in the order I think makes the most sense, but feel free to start wherever you think will help the most.

The first eight chapters are **The Story**. This is a fictional narrative of a group of leaders from different sectors and demographics who come together to understand how to solve culture problems in their own organizations, and to encourage one another. None of them are "based on a true story," but they are all reasonable possibilities based on the work I've done with leaders locally, nationally, and internationally. For those who appreciate case studies or are looking for a soft entry to the tool, this is the best starting point.

The next six chapters are **The Elements**. These are more direct explanations of what Reason, Energy, Alignment, Clarity, and Trust look like in an organization. They give specific descriptions and approaches for dealing with issues. You'll also understand the importance and power of skilled Celebration. Leaders who want the content without unnecessary embellishment will find what they're looking for here. These chapters fill in the gaps from the narrative and serve as a resource to come back to and deepen your understanding.

Finally, the last thing in the book is **The User's Guide**. This is the nitty-gritty of the steps to take to use The REACTION Dashboard alone or with a group. It's the basic system for getting the most out of the tool in a practical way. Placed at the very end for easy reference, this is where you can go to remind yourself of the specific things you can do to build a healthy culture for yourself and your entire organization.

<u>My hope for you</u>

Maybe you've been part of unhealthy organizations. You know how demotivating it is to believe in what you're doing and give an honest effort—but still feel drained and discouraged. You've experienced the frustration of pushing against a tide of indifference or negativity. You've lived the very real cost of dysfunction.

I've seen too many good people and high potential organizations fall apart despite solid strategy and a commitment to execution. It happens all the time. Unhealthy cultures sap energy, spoil effort, and steal effectiveness. Lasting greatness depends on maintaining a healthy culture.

Hopefully you've also been in situations where the culture was amazing. You know the sense of momentum, energy, and optimism that supersedes circumstances. You've been part of a team or group who lived in the synergy of great dynamics. It's meaningful, effective, and fun.

Now as a leader you want to build that better culture (and avoid the worse one!). You know that in some way it's your job to make your organization a positive and productive one for everyone involved. And you may be frustrated that the best strategy and execution techniques aren't getting that done.

This book is for you.

The REACTION Dashboard is a tool you can learn quickly, apply immediately, repeat continually, and see working right in front of your eyes. With a little effort on your part it can become a key tool in your leadership kit.

Leadership is hard enough. Having a way to demystify culture and do something about it in real time can mean the difference between confidence and insecurity for you and for your followers.

I wish you great success and great understanding in your life and leadership. I hope that The REACTION Dashboard helps you do just that.

# The Story

## Chapter One – An Uncertain Beginning

Stacy could see that Jim was impressed. She smiled proudly but then focused again on the conversation going on around them. She found it hard to scribble fast enough to keep up with all the notes she wanted to take as the group shared their thoughts, questions, and insights.

And to think they had only come that night to encourage a friend.

That friend, Neil Tinley, had been a student at Valleyside High during the time that Stacy had been the vice-principal there. He had been an insightful, if academically unremarkable student, who was involved in several activities and sports, and who was known for bringing interesting perspectives to class discussions. He seemed to have a knack for fitting in at the edges of a variety of social circles, understanding the unspoken expectations of each clique and club.

And now he was challenging and inspiring this group of established leaders.

Stacy had been pleased a few years later when he had applied and been hired as an intern working with her husband, Jim, at their church. She remembered what Jim had said about Neil's internship interview: Neil had been so nervous that Jim had very nearly hired someone else. Now, she couldn't help marvel at the difference in the way Neil confidently managed this group of twenty engaged adults.

This evening had begun with an email invitation. Now the director of a youth camp a couple hours away, Neil had been working on understanding how organizations work and how they could work better, and was hoping to gather some people to share what he'd come up with. The invitation went out to about 50 people. Jim was going to decline but Stacy had pushed for them to accept.

"Come on, Jim," she'd said, "Neil has always been really bright and you always talk about the importance of encouraging young leaders.

Besides, we could both use some new ideas in our organizations these days."

That was certainly true. Life Point Church had been plateaued for too long and Jim wasn't the only one feeling it. A couple of core families had left and some others seemed restless. Nothing was really wrong; things had just grown somehow stale and nothing Jim did was making any difference.

Stacy's situation was more dynamic. She'd been transferred to Forest Secondary at the start of that year after four good years as principal across town. Forest had a reputation as a tough school, but even so she was surprised at how dysfunctional it really was. Students, staff, teachers and administration couldn't seem to agree on anything, and the tension and factions made meaningful progress next to impossible. Most days Stacy was exhausted at her desk by 10 a.m. Nothing in her experience had prepared her for a challenge like this.

The twenty or so people in the room seemed fully engaged in the discussion after only a few brief introductions. Stacy had been pleasantly surprised to see Neil's father, Brad, in the back row. Brad was a supportive and loving man but he seemed to find it hard to understand his son spending the early years of what could be a profitable career "working for peanuts at summer camp like a teenager." It didn't fit the expectations the high-performing corporate executive had for someone with his son's obvious leadership potential.

Neil was talking. "So, my conviction is that what we've been missing as leaders is a way to improve organizational culture. Strategy and problem solving are always going to be important, but culture is the thing that can really make an organization great."

"I remember reading that culture eats strategy for breakfast," said someone from the other side of the room. Stacy recognized her as a young entrepreneur who was starting up a small chain of outdoor activity stores and clubs called Go Out And Play.

Neil was copying the phrase onto the whiteboard. "Exactly, Nina! That's it. The challenge has been in finding a useful way to understand culture, and then to figure out what we can do to make it better. That's what I want to run by all of you for your feedback this evening. It looks like this..."

The worksheet Neil handed around was a simple one with the title The REACTION Dashboard at the top of the page. Beneath that was a blank chart, with six rows and four columns. If not for Neil's energy, Stacy might have felt a little let down by the sheer blankness of it.

When everyone had a paper, Neil wrote words on the whiteboard and explained what he was doing. "We label the rows as Elements of Culture, starting with Reason, then Energy, Alignment, Clarity, and at the bottom Trust."

"So the anagram is REACT—like a chemical reaction? Nice." Stacy didn't recognize the middle-aged man who made the observation, but she appreciated how quickly he picked up on the connection between the first letters.

"It actually goes a little further than that," Neil said with a grin. "You can label the columns with the titles Individual, Organization, and Network. So it really does complete the word REACTION."

There were a few pleased chuckles as the group filled in their charts to match Neil's.

|           | Individual | Organization | Network | Special |
|-----------|------------|--------------|---------|---------|
| Reason    |            |              |         |         |
| Energy    |            |              |         |         |
| Alignment |            |              |         |         |
| Clarity   |            |              |         |         |
| Trust     |            |              |         |         |

Over the next thirty minutes they went through the worksheet as an exercise. First they filled in each box with a score from 1-10 (10 representing the best possible reality) given the current situation in their own workplace. Neil guided them with explanations for each Element, and several from the group added their own examples or asked clarifying questions. There was a noticeable buzz in the room as they all completed the final box and looked to the front again.

|  | Individual | Organization | Network | Special |
|---|---|---|---|---|
| Reason | 9 | 8 | 7 | 8 |
| Energy | 7 | 6 | 8 | 8 |
| Alignment | 9 | 9 | 9 | 9 |
| Clarity | 6 | 8 | 7 | 6 |
| Trust | 9 | 8 | 8 | 9 |

"Excuse me, Neil." It was Brad. "This is an interesting exercise, and I do appreciate the value of considering the subjective sense we each have of our organizational cultures. But so what? How does this make a difference tomorrow morning to the hundreds of people and millions of dollars I am responsible for?" The question sounded sincere, but the effect was instantly draining.

Neil, however, was totally unfazed, "You're exactly right! If we stop here, all we've done is entertained ourselves for a little while. I was raised to know that leadership has to have an impact—right, Dad?" There was generous laughter before Neil took the next step.

"Look at your worksheet. You've recorded 15 numbers, but those are just data points until we put them back into context. If we stopped here, it would be like driving a car by only staring at the dashboard—you'd crash and probably sooner than later. We need to use our windows and mirrors. So the next step is to do what most leaders do best: look for some problems to solve."

The next few minutes were engaged with identifying which two entries on the REACTION dashboard represented immediate danger or potential damage, what Neil called Warning Lights. These were marked with triangles on the worksheet and then Neil demonstrated a simple approach for ensuring that the process of solving these problems was underway, even if the solutions themselves weren't yet apparent. Stacy was actually surprised at how well the tool clarified issues below the surface that needed attention, and prepared her to deal with them before they became worse.

|           | Individual | organization | Network | Special |
|-----------|------------|--------------|---------|---------|
| Reason    | 9          | 8            | 7       | 8       |
| Energy    | 7          | 6            | 8       | 8       |
| Alignment | 9          | 9            | 9       | 9       |
| Clarity   | 6          | 8            | 7       | 6       |
| Trust     | 9          | 8            | 8       | 9       |

"Okay," Neil said. "That was the easy part. As we've said, leaders like to solve problems. Some of you have probably been accused of causing problems if there aren't any at times, just to have something to do". Stacy elbowed Jim, and he had to smile.

"What I'm learning is that, for many leaders, the more difficult, and probably the more impactful task is not more problem-solving, but celebration."

Neil paused, and it seemed like everyone else did too. Stacy glanced quickly around. A few people were smiling, a couple frowned, most looked surprised and a little curious which was exactly how she felt.

"I know celebration isn't the first leadership skill that comes to mind for most of us, and I'm not saying it's more crucial than any other. But I am saying that I'm coming to believe it's a skill that has been largely neglected, has potential for massive impact, and can be accomplished by any leader at relatively little expense."

**Celebration is a skill that has been largely neglected but it has the potential for massive impact!**

He went on to explain that when he began learning about organizational culture, the idea of celebration wasn't even remotely on his radar, but that the more he researched and reflected, the more he became convinced that there is something significant and powerful that can be accomplished through the strategic skill of celebration. More heads were nodding along with him now, but Stacy noticed that Jim looked skeptical, and, when she snuck a glance over her shoulder, Brad seemed uncertain as well.

# The REACTION Dashboard

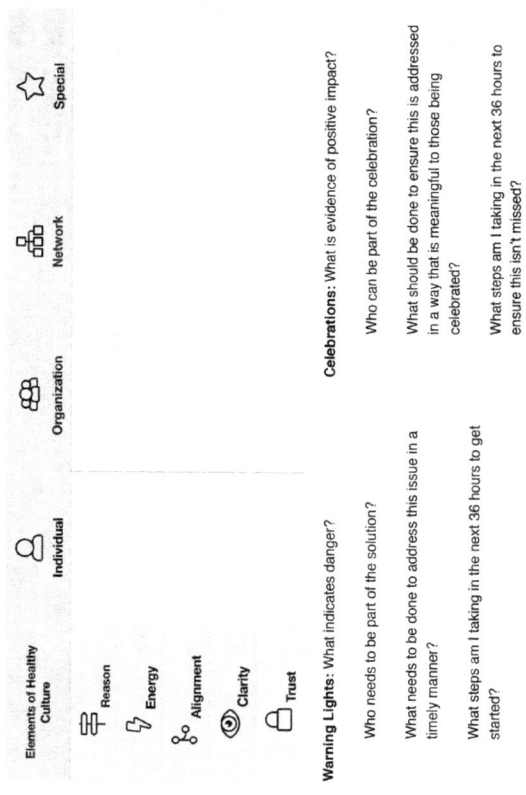

## Chapter Two – Celebration?!?

"When I say celebration, I'm not talking about party hats and cupcakes on your birthday," Neil said quickly. "Celebration is as strategic and relevant as budget and buildings—or at least it can and should be".

Now people were listening.

"That's a bold claim, my friend." It was the same man who had so quickly recognized the acronym REACT. "You're going to have to convince me of this one." The challenge seemed to be given with sincere courtesy, but it clearly reflected the thoughts of many in the room.

"Of course, Amir. I'd expect no less from you, or any serious leader." Neil's response was confident. "May I pick on you for a minute?".

A smile and consenting nod gave Neil permission to plunge forward. "You've just come into your role leading Hope Springs, our regional mental health network. Before you started, you surely spent some time adding to your knowledge of the field by learning about the specifics of this organization and the news of the community."

Amir shrugged. "Of course."

"But as qualified as you are, and as well-prepared as you were when you walked in on your first day, there were things you just couldn't possibly understand until you were actually in the organization. There's jargon, inside jokes, personalities, common habits, unspoken history, and so much more about working at Hope Springs that would never show up on a balance sheet or annual report. And I'd bet that those are the things that are most challenging for a leader coming in from the outside."

"You've been reading my journal," Amir replied after a slightly self-conscious pause.

"That's it. That's culture." Neil was really warming up now. "And the key to understanding and affecting culture isn't something you can do effectively from the outside. You have to become part of it, marinate in it, and then progressively, incrementally, you can work to adjust the culture if you can identify things that can be improved. That's what REACTION is all about."

"Okay, you've found my felt need," admitted Amir as several others nodded. "But you haven't connected culture to celebration so I'm still a little skeptical."

"Fair enough," Neil conceded. "Most of us learned leadership in a way that was focused on efficiency and strategy. We've had SMART goals drilled into us and learned dozens of ways to motivate people. We've read the books, attended the conferences, and completed the courses. But we know there's something missing in all of that. Our favourite work and even volunteer situations engaged us at a deeper level so that even years later we look back on them with an uncommon appreciation. You might even dare to call it joy."

Neil paused, and then addressed the entire group. "What are the most magical, meaningful moments in all of your work history? Think of the story of the most satisfying moments you've ever experienced at work or while volunteering."

Jim spoke up. "Do you mean our greatest achievements? Like when we raised all the money for the missions project in Haiti?"

"That was amazing," Neil replied. Stacy knew that Neil had been working at the church at that time and he could remember it. "But I'm looking for something more specific right now. When you look back on that project, tell us about the most powerful moment of the whole campaign. Describe as vividly as you can your personal highlight of that achievement."

"Hmmm...all right. I'll give it a shot." Jim was uncharacteristically hesitant. "Okay, if I'm really honest, the amazing moment was the Sunday when the congregation brought their donations in. We'd been public about it for weeks, and we spent months before that, designing the whole thing. It was a big deal for us to attempt something so big, especially for another country. There were several times when I wondered if we'd aimed too high, stretched our folks too far, asked too much. I lost some sleep the night before, I admit."

Jim paused, and swallowed hard. Stacy quietly took his hand.

"When the time in the service came for people to bring their gifts forward and present them to God and the church, the response was overwhelming. Even the people who had been resistant to the whole campaign were coming to the front with envelopes in their hands. We were all surprised by the response. People were laughing and clapping—it was really out of character for our reserved style. I was standing there, totally amazed by what was happening, and then our children's program leader nudged me aside and stepped to the podium. She announced that the kids had raised nearly $600. Actually I remember exactly how much it was— $584.58—from their own activities over the month. I hadn't even thought of involving them. They did it all on their own. Looking at those kids with their bags of change and the biggest smiles just made it for me. To think that they were getting a taste for caring for others and experiencing the joy of giving. That was just so fantastic! I don't know if I'll ever have another moment like that as long as I'm a pastor."

Jim wasn't the only with tears in his eyes as he finished.

"Wow! Thanks." Neil was caught up in his own memory of that event. "You know, as amazing as that was, my highlight of that project was totally different. I happened to be coming down the office hall when the finance team finished counting the donations that afternoon and overheard them talking. When Julia finished adding it all up she gave the total to Raphael, and he made her repeat it twice, just to confirm the number. I couldn't see either of them from the hall but the wonder and excitement in their voices has always stayed with me. They were the first to know we'd doubled our goal and it seemed like they wanted to just sit with that number for a moment and let it sink in before they came out and made the announcement to everyone else."

"You know, I never knew that. I never even thought about what that must have been like for them." Jim had a wide smile on his face. "I guess I thought everyone's highlight would be the same as mine."

"In some ways they are very much the same, Jim, but we'll get to that in a few minutes. I think we've warmed things up enough now for everyone to share their own highlight stories with someone sitting nearby."

The next several minutes were abuzz with happy, reflective, and often emotional storytelling. When he was ready to pull the group back together, Neil had some difficulty getting people's attention. It seemed like when people got talking about these special moments they wanted to linger in the feelings.

When he did regain attention, it was an eager and engaged group who were ready for what came next. What followed was a discussion of the traits of a major highlight moment. Answers varied, but in every case there was a sense of meaningful accomplishment, recognition of effort, and progress toward something of value.

"So," Neil prodded, "if these moments are so powerful for us, wouldn't it make sense for us to be intentional about identifying and recognizing every bit of evidence of progress that happens in our organizations, and making it easier for everyone involved to celebrate them?"

"Of course it would," said Nina. "I'd love for the new staff I'm hiring to catch the excitement of what Go Out and Play is doing. But how do I know which things to celebrate? And how can we do it with all the time and budget limits we're already dealing with?"

Neil paused for a moment before answering. He glanced at his watch. "You know, Nina, that's something I'm still trying to figure out myself, and for the team at camp where I work. I'd love to tell you I know how to do this, but right now I'm just not confident that I do. I have a lot more learning to do, and tonight has been so helpful. And I also see that we're out of time tonight. I am so grateful to all of you for coming and hearing me out on these ideas while they're still coming together. I hope it's been useful to you…"

"Hang on a second, Neil." Every head turned to see Stacy standing up and interrupting her former student. "This is really good stuff, and it has already helped me think through some of the challenges at Forest Secondary in a different way, a way I think is going to make a real difference. But I think there's a lot more to this than you might even realize. I'm wondering if maybe I'm not alone in wanting to dig deeper into REACTION and how it can help my organization. How would you feel about a group of us getting together a few more times to see what else we can learn?"

Before Neil had a chance to say anything a couple more people spoke up with their desire to keep the conversation going. By the time Neil had gathered his things and was headed to his small station wagon, Stacy, Jim, Amir, and Nina had committed to coming back in a few weeks to explore the potential of REACTION for their own organizations.

It was an unusually diverse group:

Stacy, the principal of a tough public high school.

Jim, the long term pastor of a prominent local church.

Amir, the newly hired Executive Director of the regional mental health network.

Nina, the enthusiastic entrepreneur.

All gathered by Neil, the insightful young camp director.

Brad spoke up. "Would you mind if I joined your group for the next discussion? I think there may be something I can learn from you about this culture and celebration stuff."

Stacy could see conflicting emotions flicker across Neil's face. She knew if she were Neil, she might feel a little intimidated having his father, a successful corporate executive join the group. As for her, though, Stacy left feeling inspired and eager to keep thinking about REACTION.

# Chapter Three – Reason

Despite replies confirming the follow-up sessions, Neil wondered if the other leaders would show up to dig deeper into the potential the REACTION dashboard had for improving their organizations. Seeing other cars already in the parking lot when he arrived and everyone seated and chatting a few minutes before they were scheduled to begin made him both a little nervous and excited about where the conversations would take them.

He began by passing out the simple worksheet to the other five. "I think we can be most helpful if we start by reviewing the basics of REACTION and then explore things further together." Everyone agreed and they set to work.

"Can you quickly remind me of what each of the elements of culture are?" Amir asked.

"Of course. Try thinking of it like this." Neil wrote on the whiteboard he'd set up:

Reason: Why we're doing everything we do.

Energy: The capacity to do the work.

Alignment: Everybody pulling in the same direction.

Clarity: Knowing my part.

Trust: Being able to rely on the people and organization.

"Now we just rate each of the elements on a 10-point scale, 10 being highest, first for ourselves as the Individual, then for the Organization as a whole, and then for our Network, right?" Nina clearly remembered the ease of the approach from last time and people quickly added numbers to their pages.

"When you say Organization, who exactly does that mean?" Stacy asked. "Is it all my teachers, staff, and students? What about the board office, or parents and community leaders?"

"And for the Health Network, does Organization include our clients?" Amir added.

"There are hundreds of employees at Green Leaf Inc." Brad chipped in. "I really can't know how all of them feel about these things. And I'm not sure who all to include in Network either. There are so many different clients, partners, suppliers, competitors, contractors, and government entities we interact with regularly. They have very different dynamics."

"Good points," Neil acknowledged. "I don't think this tool is meant to address every particular relationship or situation in detail. It's more of an overview that helps us figure out where to focus our attention and effort. So what working definitions of Organization and Network are most useful in a real way?"

Discussion ranged for several minutes with each person seeing differences in their own situation. After a series of suggestions, revisions, and backtracks, eventually they settled on what they called useful descriptions rather than definitions, recognizing the uniqueness of each role and organization.

Neil wiped off the whiteboard and wrote their descriptions down:

Individual: The person using the REACTION tool.

Organization: The people I can influence significantly. The entire team in a smaller organization. Those at my level, reporting to me, and those I report to in a large or complex organization.

Network: All the stakeholders who influence or are influenced by our organization. A diverse group in most cases that may include clientele/customers, suppliers, investors/donors, partner organizations, unions, government, community organizations, media, outside consultants, industry organizations, competitors, former staff/alumni, contractors, and an almost endless variety of contacts.

"I'm still struggling with Network," Jim admitted. "There are so many different groups connected to each of our organizations. We can't be attentive to all of them. At any given time there are some that are more important to us, or that need to be."

"I agree, Jim," said Stacy. "Perhaps we could add a column on the sheet for a particular subset of the Network that we think needs particular focus for some reason."

"Let's call it Special!" Amir was grinning. "That way the anagram still works: REACTIONS instead of REACTION." Chuckles and smiles from the group made it official and the optional Special column was added to the worksheet.

Neil was pleased to see others building on his original design. "I wonder if our next step could be to see how the tool actually helps in a real situation. Does anyone have a particularly concerning score that we could look at together?"

"I hate to be pushy, but I do and I'd love your help." Amir spoke to the group. "Since taking over at Hope Springs, I've been frustrated by the way things have been going. People seem half-hearted in their work, and it seems like there's not enough pride in what we do. I mean, there's so much good stuff happening, but we don't talk about it and too many of our people seem like they used to have a sense of great purpose but now they see their work as just a job. I didn't have a clear sense of what was wrong, but I've got low scores all over the Organization column. I think you called them Warning Lights last time, and that's exactly what it feels like, a warning. I fear that if we don't do something about this, there is real danger ahead for us."

"Thanks for being so up front, Amir." Neil said what everyone was thinking. "Let's see what we can come up with to help."

After a thoughtful pause, Jim spoke up. "What you're describing sounds similar to some issues we're having at the church. I can understand how that feels. Of the Warning Lights for Hope Springs, which one seems most concerning?"

Now it was Amir's turn to pause. "I'd have to say it's a Reason issue at heart." he said after thinking for a minute. "Our people don't seem burned out and they know their parts in what we do. No one seems to be doing their own thing or wasting much effort. And I think they trust one another. We've just lost the sense of why we're doing all this work in the first place somehow."

"Okay, so what do the rest of us do to keep the Reason for our work in the forefront of people's minds?" Neil was sure there was some insight to be found in the gathered leaders.

At first there was some hesitance to risk being perceived as more expert than others, but with some prodding, ideas began to flow. Eventually the whiteboard was covered with ways other organizations had handled this challenge.

"I have to constantly remind myself to constantly remind everyone else of our Reason," Jim said. "It's so easy to assume we all know why we're here, and let the enthusiasm and focus slowly slip away. That's why I love that we have communion every Sunday. It forces me to make sure that whatever Scripture or sermon topic I'm teaching on, I have to come back to the heart of our faith every week. I need that for myself and several of our people have told me how much they appreciate it."

"Great example," said Nina. "I'm not religious, but I get the idea. I think that's why I named my company Go Out and Play, and put our logo on everything we can. It's not just marketing. I truly believe we have a message, an invitation really, for our whole community."

Amir looked up from his notes. "This is very helpful. I see some common themes in what you all have shared. May I use to board to show you what I'm hearing?"

Amir had shown himself to have a knack for pulling ideas together in a way others could grasp so everyone agreed. Amir wrote in silence for a minute or two and then stepped back so they all could see.

"It seems to me that what I need to do is continually reinforce what we are about as an organization serving those in our community affected by mental health issues. Based on the examples you've offered I can start with 5 S's: a slogan, a story, a statistic, a symbol, and a strategy. I think many of these are already available to me, but putting them all together and using them well could potentially turn things around. I've got an all-staff day in two-weeks' time and I'm going to use my part of that day to share our Reason like this."

### 5 S's for Communicating Reason
**Slogan, Story, Statistic, Symbol, Strategy**

For another twenty minutes or so they helped Amir gather his thoughts for the Reason presentation and then headed home, looking forward to the next time together.

**Case Study: Notes for Amir's Hope Springs All-Staff Meeting**

Slogan: Here to Help, Hope to Heal

Story: Jason and Jasmine

-Years lost to depression

-Difficult decision to ask for help

-Key people and programs

-Hope for the future

What story do you tell yourself to remind you why we do this?

Statistic: We know the prevalence of mental health and addiction issues in our communities. We know that things we do make a real difference for many of those suffering and their families. Still 42% of people in our community are unsure if they would socialize with someone who has a mental illness. We can't help people who won't ask and people won't ask if admitting the struggle means their friends will abandon them. We are going to change the stigma.

Symbol: Pocket-sized springs. We help people who are bent, stretched, and pressured, to return to their true shape.

Strategy:

Grassroots awareness campaign beginning immediately

Public campaign to follow in 6 months

Story sharing on intraweb

Departmental meetings will include 5 S's

## Chapter Four – Energy

The next time they met, the group was eager to hear how Amir's staff-day presentation on Reason had gone, and asked him about it even before Neil had the flip chart and whiteboard in place.

"I have to say, it was one of the most encouraging days I've had since coming to Hope Springs," Amir said with confidence. "Not only that, but several of my team came up to me afterward and told me they hadn't been this fired up about what we do in years. They all had their own stories of clients and families we've served that remind them of our Reason. And I've seen those little springs on desks and even being carried around by staff at every level of the organization!"

"So it was a complete success!" Nina encouraged.

"Well, yes and no," Amir replied. "I had two managers approach their supervisors and say that they weren't really sure that they care as deeply about serving our community as everyone else seems to. We think one of them just needs some time to come on side; she has a lot of other things going in her life that make it hard to fully commit.

"But the other is probably going to have to go. The truth is, he probably should have transitioned out of our work some time ago from what I'm told. The Reason conversation just crystallized what was apparent but being overlooked. In a way, even that is a kind of success. And we know now the importance of making our Reason a core part of hiring or promoting his replacement."

**Why we exist – our Reason – should be a core part of hiring and promoting.**

As the group discussed Amir's experience Neil handed out blank REACTION sheets, with the added Special column based on their last time together.

With little prompting, each leader began filling in the grid, occasionally voicing an observation or question to refresh their understanding of one of the boxes.

When they had finished it was Jim who spoke up. "Would I be jumping ahead to ask for insight from the group on some issues at the church that are even more clear as I do my chart?"

"Go ahead," said Neil. "That's what we're here for, and I think we'll all learn better with a real-life scenario to consider."

With nods from the rest, Jim began, "It's the Energy row. Over the last six months I've been taking my health more seriously, with Stacy's strong encouragement. I'm eating better, getting more sleep, and being consistently active. I even ran in a local 10k race last month. I've changed some other habits too, and I feel more spiritually vital than I have in a long time. My Energy level is the highest it's been in years. I feel ready to take on something big.'

"Sounds like a Celebration is in order. Well done." Brad raised his coffee in salute.

"Thanks. The thing is that the Energy level among the church leaders and congregation is the opposite. They believe in what we're trying to do at Life Point, but they just don't have it in them to engage the way we need to, to get there right now."

Neil interjected. "Let me make a quick observation: Brad is right that your improved health and Energy is something to be celebrated. I really think you need to be sure to not miss the chance to do so. Like we've said, leaders tend to not celebrate enough."

"We actually do have something planned." Stacy spoke up. "We hadn't really described it as a celebration but we're going to hike the Grand Canyon in a few months. We've talked about it for years, but now we're fit enough to actually do it and enjoy it."

"You'll love it!" Nina enthused. "There's nothing like it. I went there during college and still have a couple pics above my desk."

A couple others added their congratulations to Jim and shared their own experiences or dreams of the American landmark before Neil directed them back to the topic at hand.

"Okay, Jim, tell us more about the Energy issue you're seeing."

"It's actually not really a new thing. It's probably been slipping for a couple years when I think about it, but as my energy level is rising, it becomes a lot more apparent. With all the busyness in people's lives these days, they just seem worn out. They show up, even lead programs, but the extra effort it takes to have the kind of impact we want isn't there. Or at least I'm not seeing it."

Amir asked a typically insightful question: "Is the issue that they aren't bringing much energy to your organization, the church, or that they just don't have much energy for anything at all?"

"I'm not sure," Jim responded.

"Because it seems to me," elaborated Amir, "that there is a big difference between people not choosing to give effort to your organization and them not having any energy to give even if they want to."

"People can't give what they don't have," Stacy mused, and everyone nodded. "So when we talk about Energy, are we talking about people having it, or them bringing it to work?"

Neil jumped in. "I've been thinking about this and I think it's really a combination of both. The phrase I've been considering is Maximum Sustainable Discretionary Effort."

"You're going to have to break that one down for me, Neil," Brad interrupted "I'm not sure I'm following you."

Neil shrugged. "Let me see if I can explain it." After writing the phrase on the whiteboard, Neil described what it meant to him. "I think what we all want, from ourselves and others, is the kind of involvement that brings out our best over time. We all know there's some minimum activity level we have to maintain to keep our jobs, but no one's really happy doing that for very long. We want to engage ourselves in something in a bigger way, for a reason we understand and care about.

"So what we want is for people to choose to give more than they have to—that's what I mean by discretionary. And we want as much more as possible—that's why I say maximum. But we can only give so much for so long before it wears us down and we just can't do it anymore. Burning people out isn't good leadership, so we really want it to be sustainable."

**Maximum Sustainable Discretionary Effort – everything our people can give without burning out**

"Sounds like what Csikszentmihalyi called Flow," Stacy added with interest. "But can we really expect to stay in such an ideal place for any length of time? I mean, it sounds great, but is it realistic?"

"Probably not," Neil admitted. "But that doesn't mean we don't aim for it. I struggle with this one at camp every summer. My young staff are unbelievably energetic when they arrive, but by the time August rolls around, most of them are so deeply exhausted they get sick, start squabbling, or just can't give our campers the quality of care and attention they deserve. We do a lot to help them manage their energy, but it really is nearly impossible."

"That may be a maturity issue on their part," Amir offered. "I've had to learn that I can't go full speed all the time. There are seasons when I do more than I can sustain, and seasons when I need to recover a little. I'm getting better at planning for that, and knowing what actually energizes me."

"That's a really good point," Stacy agreed. "We don't all gain energy from the same things. It's like in those personality profiles we sometimes do. Filling our tanks looks quite different from one person to another."

For a few minutes the group talked about the successful and unsuccessful ways they had tried to manage their energy over the years.

Then Jim raised another issue. "All this really helps, but as Amir said earlier, it's not just about people having energy—they also have to choose where to use it. And it's not only work that drains energy. One of our church board members is dealing with cancer, our administrator is directing a play at the local theatre, and our custodian is going through a messy divorce. None of them are fulfilling their roles at a high level right now, and I'm not sure it's fair to expect them to."

Brad spoke up. 'We don't have separate energy tanks for work, family, friends, hobbies, volunteering, or whatever. Though sometimes we try to act like we do. When one aspect of our lives is draining us it eventually has to impact the other areas."

"So then, how do we lead people when their energy, and ours, which is so crucial, is so variable?" Neil asked. Discussion took off and Neil tracked key insights on the whiteboard. In a few minutes they had a handful of key ideas.

Fill the Tank: We can help people figure out how to refresh and expand their energy. Physical health is a key component, but personality profiles also give great insights into the best strategies for each individual.

Seasons: Energy demands aren't consistent; they ebb and flow according to a variety of factors. We need to build times of recovery into our calendar, and regular rituals or habits that prepare us for the needs we face.

One Tank: There is a lot more to all of us than our work. We divide our energy among all the aspects of our lives. Life can vary significantly and unexpectedly in what it requires of us. We have to recognize the complexity of our lives and those of our team and community.

Misfits: Sometimes the energy-needs of a role are just more than a person can meet. If that continues over time it is necessary to change either the role or the person filling it.

Strategic Self-care: The line between self-care and self-indulgence is hard to identify. We need to have strategies for increasing our capacity and for managing immediate stress.

Neil stepped away from the board and looked at Jim. "I think this is good stuff, but does it give you any help with the specific Warning Lights you've identified at the church?"

"Actually it does." Jim looked thoughtful. "For one thing, our people have been trying to go too hard for too long. They're tired. We need to take some time to recover before taking on anything big. I can help our core team by exploring the particular ways each of them can be refreshed, and the habits they need to put in place to both rest up now and expand their energy for the future. And I can do some teaching on these themes for the whole congregation in an upcoming sermon series. This conversation has given me some key ideas that I think can really help. In fact, I'm getting energized about helping our people learn to manage their own energy."

Together they helped Jim lay out the first steps of his plan, and then each member of the group set their own action steps from the REACTION dashboard before scheduling the next session. They were all excited about how things were going and the potential for further insights.

# Chapter Five – Alignment

As the group gathered again, each leader took the same seats they had become accustomed to filling. Only Brad's was empty when it was time to begin. Neil let people continue to chat casually about the ways each was trying to apply the REACTION insights to their life and leadership. When another ten minutes had passed, Neil suggested they begin.

"Honestly, I'm not surprised Dad's not here yet," Neil began. "He's got a lot on his plate and he seems to be forever rushing from one urgent situation to another."

Sympathetic responses from the others were interrupted by Brad bustling in with an apology and taking his seat. "Sorry, gang. Sorry, Neil. I was in so many meetings today and then had to make several calls on the way over. All that and I'm honestly not sure if any of it was productive. I actually got lost on the way here I was so distracted, can you believe it? Anyway, I am sorry, but I'm here now. What are we talking about?"

His rush of words left them all out of breath.

"I'm sure we can all relate, Brad. We're glad you're here," Jim said as Neil handed out the familiar REACTION worksheets. After a few minutes of thoughtful work the boxes were filled in and all attention turned once again to Neil.

"We didn't plan it this way, but the issues raised by Amir and Jim the last two meetings conveniently addressed the first two elements, Reason and Energy. I'm wondering if we can continue the trend. Does anyone have Warning Lights in the Alignment row?"

There was a quiet moment as everyone checked their sheets and it appeared that no one saw Alignment as their most pressing need.

Then Nina spoke up. "I could be wrong Brad, but with the way you described your day I can't help but wonder if Alignment might be an area you could look into."

Brad looked surprised. A defensive expression crossed his face, but then he softened and spoke in a sincere tone. "I don't think so, Nina. What makes you say that?"

"I don't know much about leading in a huge organization like Green Leaf. I'm sure there really are a ton of different things you need to do, but if I understand Alignment properly, it's a way to ensure that all the Energy we put in as leaders is making progress towards the Reason. It doesn't sound like today worked out that way for you."

Brad looked thoughtful. After a couple moments he looked down on his sheet again and crossed out a number.

"You know what, Nina, I think you're right. I guess I'm just so used to working hard, juggling so many things, and not seeing much connection to the most meaningful results that I've become kind of numb to it. The machine just keeps cranking and it's all I can do to not get swamped."

Stacy spoke up, "I'm sure we all feel that way at times, Brad. No shame here. And since Alignment is the next element of REACTION, why don't we dig into it this time and see how it helps you, and the rest of us as well."

"Sounds good," Brad replied, "Okay, Neil, what have you got for us on Alignment?"

Neil nodded and drew a straight line on the whiteboard. At one end he wrote Reason and at the other, Energy. "Perfect Alignment would be when every bit of Energy is being applied in a direct vector towards the Reason. Nothing is lost along the way. Every action, email, meeting, and conversation is productive and worthwhile."

"And rainbow unicorns deliver cotton candy flowers to employees every hour on the hour, right?" Amir said with a laugh, and was joined by all the others.

"Okay, I admit that's more than a little idealistic," Neil acknowledged. "So let's talk about the real world. What percentage of your energy at work in the last week do you think has been expended toward the Reason?"

That began a rich discussion about productivity, technology, processes, regulations, and annoying colleagues. By the time they each came up with a number to express their percentage of aligned effort, there was a frustrated tone to their comments.

"Whoa!" Nina sighed. "You'd think as the boss in a small company I'd be spending all my time on things that keep us moving forward. I mean, I'm in charge, right? But this is actually discouraging."

"You said it!" replied Jim. "And I hate to think what the numbers would be like for the rest of our staff and core volunteers. Looking at it like this shows just how inefficient we really are."

"Could it be that leaders are the exception when it comes to this?" Stacy's tone showed she was exploring a different angle. "I mean, the teachers at school spend the majority of their time either directly working with students or preparing lessons. Volunteers at our church are hands-on with our various programs and ministries. Your staff at Go Out And Play are out on the trails or rivers all the time, Nina. But as leaders, we have to manage the strategic and operational aspects that keep all that great stuff happening. Maybe it's just harder for leaders to align our energy to the reason."

**The farther we are from the front lines of the operation, the harder it can be to see the connection between Energy and Reason.**

"Wow; that never occurred to me." Neil was intrigued. "Let's explore that for a few minutes..."

A highly engaged discussion followed about the role of leadership, the demands of management, the value of effective administration, and the relentless grind of keeping an organization moving.

It was Brad who summed it up: "So the farther we are from the front lines of the operation, the harder it can be to see the connection between Energy and Reason, but the more important it is for us to be Aligned. It probably won't look the same as for other folks, but knowing which of our activities are truly relevant is key to leading with Alignment."

Everyone agreed.

"So that's my issue," Brad continued. "I can't connect a lot of the things I do on a day-to-day basis with what Green Leaf is trying to accomplish. I bet most of my peers and our middle managers feel the same, at least some of the time. But what do I do about it? I can't just stop doing the things that don't seem to fit. I'm responsible for them, and I'm held highly accountable for them, too."

Sympathetic murmuring was interrupted by Amir. "Maybe you're using the wrong scoresheet."

Brad and most of the rest of the group looked confused.

"I'm thinking that maybe the things you're held accountable to are the problem. Let me try to explain. In my last organization, we spent a lot of time dealing with employees who had performance issues. There were too many who were below grade, time after time. For a long time, we tried to motivate them better with various combinations of carrot and stick, bonuses and demotions, even letting people go. Eventually a new manager came to me and asked a question that totally changed my perspective."

"Sounds like a magic question. What was it?" Brad was obviously intrigued.

"She asked me what she was supposed to be measuring." Amir smiled at the memory. "She told me that she had several different metrics for evaluating staff performance, and she didn't know which was most important or even how some of them related to our purpose as an organization, or Reason as we're calling it here. As we talked it became clear that we had built a system that tracked metrics that were only loosely connected to our core results, and that left people unsure what they were striving for. It took nearly a year to dig through the mess we'd made and fix it. We had to identify the most important behaviours that drove results, and focus on them in a way that made them tangible for everyone in the organization. And we had to apologize to the staff for making it so hard for them to succeed."

"So you're saying too much measurement is a problem?" Stacy was thinking about all the metrics used in the education system.

"I suppose too much of anything is a problem," Amir replied. "But in this case it wasn't just the amount of measurement. It was that we didn't truly know what we should be measuring or how to do it for each aspect of the organization. We didn't understand at a leadership level how to know what was properly aligned and what wasn't. Overcoming that challenge was what gave me the confidence to apply for my new role here."

Encouraged by the group, Amir stepped up to the whiteboard and led a brief exercise in identifying the most relevant activities to productivity, and understanding how to evaluate them. Soon everyone was rapidly making notes, interspersed with periods of concentrated reflection.

Jim commented that part of leading with Alignment meant taking the time to explore some possibilities that might not prove fruitful. That sparked another spirited discussion about the importance of creativity and innovation, and the risks of spending too much time exploring.

Neil looked at his watch and spoke with concern. "Speaking of spending too much time on something, I totally lost track of time. We're already well past schedule. I know this is going to take some work for me, and I need to involve other people from the camp to help get it right. I can see why it took a year for you, Amir. Does anyone have a final thought before we wrap up for the evening?"

Brad cleared his throat. "This is really helpful for me. You were right, Nina. I do have an Alignment issue and I think some of this conversation can help me start to address it. But it's going to have to involve a lot more than just me. This Alignment stuff is challenging in a big organization."

"It's not so easy in a little one either," Nina teased with a smile. "We may have fewer moving parts, but they spin just as fast and we have fewer resources to keep them spinning right."

The caretaker knocked on the door, making it clear that it was time for everyone to grab their things and go.

# Chapter Six – Clarity

Some of the group hadn't even completed their Reaction worksheets at the next meeting when Nina spoke up.

"Can we talk about my Warning Lights this time? I really need some insight from you all."

The group agreed immediately.

"Thanks. Okay, so ever since we started expanding more quickly I've been frustrated, but I figured it was just typical growing pains for a small business. Last weekend things boiled over and now I don't know what to do."

"We're all here to help each other, Nina." Stacy was sympathetic. "What's going on?"

"When I started Go Out and Play, it was really just me. I led the events, contacted suppliers, arranged the displays...everything. I knew every client and they knew me. Heck, a lot of them were my friends.

"But as things started taking off, I brought other people in. At first they were mostly people I knew well who came on board as much to help me out as for anything else. It was like a family, you know. The last two years, the growth has been way more than I ever imagined. We really hit on something our community was hungry for, and the combination of great products, amazing experiences, and a fun, friendly vibe took off. I couldn't keep up and that was awesome. I was pumped to bring on more people to share this dream of a more vibrant and active city. And the people we brought on are all eager, know their stuff, and have the personality to make sure our clients love what we're doing together. They take safety seriously, and they show up on time."

"That sounds good so far," Stacy said.

Nina smiled. "It was. At first it was awesome to feel like we had this fantastic group taking this thing forward together. But there were a few little things that kept cropping up that irked me, like garbage left in our van after a hike day, or life jackets hung on the wrong hooks after a canoe session. Then it was a friend telling me that she'd loved a mountain bike clinic we offered but wished there was a group of women she could ride with regularly. I couldn't believe my staff hadn't promoted the new bike club we're launching. I can accept that a receipt gets misplaced occasionally and that everyone has a bad day once in a while, but it became a constant thing of me having to cover these details after the fact and no one else making the extra effort to bring in more business."

"I know what you mean," Jim said. "Young people just don't have the same work ethic anymore. It must be a challenge at camp for you too, Neil."

Neil looked like he was going to object but Nina responded first.

"No, Jim, that's not it. Sure, I've had some young staff who don't understand commitment, but I have the same issues with my adult staff and even a retired guy who has been leading some wild edibles and bird-watching events. It's not an age thing."

"I have to agree," Neil added. "The young people working at camp blow me away with their dedication and effort. They go above and beyond all the time to make it a great experience for the kids. I'm not saying there aren't some issues with every generation, but a lot of the stuff being said about teens and twenties these days just isn't true in my experience."

Jim apologized for his assumption and Nina continued: "So this weekend we had the most events we've ever had. It was crazy and awesome! I was flying around checking in on things and taking pictures for our web and social media sites. Everything was going so well. But when I got back to the shop ahead of the groups, I found the coolers were all completely empty. Everyone had sold drinks and snacks to their groups earlier but no one had re-stocked them, so there was nothing cold for when they got back. It may not seem like a big deal, but that time when everyone hangs around for a while after the program finishes is huge for us to build community and promote other things we're doing. The longer people hang around, the more gear they buy and the more future events they sign up for. Cold drinks are actually a big deal for me, and instead of hanging around chatting, people left to get their refreshment somewhere else. I was fuming!

"When the clients had gone, the team were heading to their cars too but I made them come back. I'm not proud of this, but I kind of lost it. I told them I was really upset that they'd left the cooler empty and that it was costing us business. I went a little overboard honestly. I said I was fed up with being the only one who really cared about Go Out and Play, and that if things didn't change I was going to start firing people. I'm not a yeller, but I sure did yell some."

"Whoa, that must have been awful," Stacy said gently "How did they respond?"

"I think mostly they were shocked. I mean all the programs had gone really well and, like I said, I'm not a yeller, so it was pretty out of character. Someone protested that he wasn't the one that left it empty. Others just looked at me like I was crazy. A couple got defensive, which I guess was understandable. Finally, one of my best people spoke in a quiet but clear tone. She said she was sorry that the biggest day in our history was ending so badly and that she hadn't re-stocked the cooler. She said that she honestly didn't know that was part of her job, but that she could see now why it's important and that she wouldn't let it happen again. It cut the tension and everyone mumbled similar apologies, but they all left deflated. It really sucked."

There was a commiserating silence for a few moments before Amir spoke. "May I suggest that what you've described is probably connected to an issue with Clarity. If your staff didn't know how important it is to have cold drinks ready at the end of the day, or that they are expected to keep the cooler full, then they may have just assumed it was someone else's problem or not a problem at all."

Nina offered a half-smile. "That's exactly what I realized as I was filling the cooler and tidying up the van after they all left. I just assumed they would know that these little things are important and they would take care of them without being told. I sat down on a bench with a lukewarm apple juice and called every last one of them and apologized before I went home. It was probably the most humbling thing I've ever done but they were almost all very gracious."

"That's amazing, Nina. I don't know if I'd ever be vulnerable enough to do that," Jim said, and everyone nodded their agreement.

"So, you dealt with the immediate issue pretty well in the end, and you may have actually made stronger relationships with your team in the end by admitting your mistakes," Neil said. "But I don't think this is really an issue about putting drinks in the cooler, is it?"

Nina sighed. "You're right, Neil. The cooler is just an example that put me over the edge on Sunday. And me losing my cool probably exposed the bigger issue of my team not understanding or embracing the whole scope of what I need them to be doing.

"The obvious solution is to update policies and role descriptions to include stocking the cooler and cleaning up the van. But I have a feeling there's more to it than just that really. I'm not really a rules person, except for safety issues, and our culture thrives on the casual feel of what we do."

"Maybe that culture has to change." Stacy spoke kindly, but pointedly. "You can have a casual tone for clients while still being professional as a staff. Policy and clear roles are a necessity to establish expectations and ensure they are understood. They may not be fun but they are like the framework that keeps the fun happening. Admittedly, at the school we've become too hung up on detailing responsibilities and procedures to the point that every little thing can feel like it requires a policy, and I'm working on that, but I've always seen policy as the string that allows the kite to fly rather than an anchor that keeps it from flying."

Everyone liked the analogy and they spent several minutes exploring it. Eventually they turned back to Nina to see if she was getting the help she needed.

"I think so. Clarity is like a kite string when we get it right. What I need to do is ensure that everyone understands and accepts all the expectations of their roles, and that they see how those expectations help them with their jobs and connect to the big picture of what we're trying to do."

**Clarity is like a kite string. It connects the specifics of people's jobs to the reason we're all working.**

"That's it!" Stacy was enthusiastic, "Shared expectations alone can't make a culture great. If people don't like the Reason, or each other, it can start to look like a list of demands instead of like the lines on the edge of the field that mark out the space where we play together. We need Clarity, especially as an organization gets bigger or more complex. But when Clarity becomes the focus, it's totally uninspiring and we just look to get the tasks done with as little hassle or effort as possible."

"That ties us back to Reason and Energy, I guess," Neil said. "These connections between the elements of culture fascinate me. I hope we can understand that more, but it is time for us to finish for the night." Neil sincerely felt amazed by the ways his simple model was so much deeper than he had imagined when he had first brought it to the group several weeks ago.

On the way out, Nina made plans to spend an evening with Stacy, working together to improve the role descriptions and policies for Go Out and Play, and figuring out how to best introduce them in a way that would help her team see them as a positive thing. Apparently sushi would be involved.

# Chapter Seven – Trust

A brisk 5k run along the lake path followed by shrimp rolls was exactly what Stacy and Nina needed to deepen the friendship that had been developing as part of Neil's group. They laughed easily and learned a lot more about each other's lives. Stacy agreed to come to Nina's next team meeting to help present the revised policies that would help prevent another "cooler catastrophe" as they were now referring to it, as well as to prepare Go Out And Play for continued growth. They sat in companionable calm for a moment before Nina asked an insightful question.

"Do you think Trust is the Warning Light for you at Forest Secondary? I mean, from what you've shared with me and the group, it's like you have good people who know what they're supposed to be doing, but they're just stuck relationally." She paused, then continued with a grin, "Besides, you're the only one we haven't picked on, and Trust is the only Element left."

Stacy could only agree, though she was somewhat dreading the discussion. The culture at Forest was bad and getting worse despite her best efforts. She was beginning to think she was too far out of her comfort zone and would never be able to turn it around.

---
---

A week later, while the others were quickly filling in their REACTION sheets, Stacy's pen sat unused on her notebook. The week since her run with Nina had sapped her of both optimism and confidence. She really didn't want to be with the group tonight; Jim had bribed her with the promise of a cappuccino on the way home, and even seeing these leaders who were becoming friends wasn't helping much.

When Neil asked if anyone had a practical issue of Trust that could serve as a case study, she could feel everyone stare at her even as she looked blankly down at her hands. It took a nudge from Nina, sitting on her right, to engage her.

"Okay. Here it is. Trust is so low at Forest that I don't even know where to start. Students don't trust teachers, teachers don't trust administration, parents don't trust the board of education, and I'm pretty sure no one trusts me. I've never been so discouraged or doubted myself so much. Twice yesterday I picked up the phone to call my superintendent and ask for a transfer out but couldn't handle admitting my failure. I'm stuck, the school's stuck, and I don't want to be there right now."

The rawness of the rush of emotion startled everyone, even her husband, who gently put his arm around her. She shrugged it off. "I'm sorry, guys. I know this REACTION thing has really helped all of you, and I'm glad. Actually I'm jealous. I've been thinking about trust since that first session when Neil introduced the dashboard, but I'm not getting anywhere. It's getting worse and nothing I've done has helped at all. If you all have any ideas for me I'd love to hear them."

After a few moments of sympathetic silence, Neil spoke: "Before we get into the specifics of your situation at school, Stacy, I wonder if we could just share some of the things we've understood about trust in our own learning and experience. That might be a way to ease into it from a different angle."

Nina began. "I've really appreciated the idea that trust is the basic currency of leadership. I think I read that description in a couple business articles. It reminds me that when I ask my people to do something new, tough, or different, I am drawing down on the amount of trust I've built up with them over the years we've worked together."

**Trust is the basic currency of leadership.**

"That reminds me of how Dad explained it to me as a kid," Neil turned to Brad. "You described trust as a piggy bank where doing things right—especially the little things—was the way to build up trust deposits, and doing things that were wrong was like withdrawals. I've always found that really helpful, and shared it with staff at camp, especially when they let me down."

Nina jumped in. "The thing with trust is that the withdrawals are usually a lot bigger than the deposits. Like when someone shows up on time for work ten times it doesn't mean as much as when they show up late just once."

Amir spoke about the insights he'd gleaned from a consultant at his previous job who had emphasized how trust works to speed up everything an organization does, while distrust grinds everything to a halt, with people second-guessing the skill and motivations of others. He reflected on how much trust had improved after he became intentional about doing little things like acknowledging the contributions of his colleagues and owning up to his mistakes. "A sincere apology has become one of my most useful, and humbling, skills," he concluded.

"I find this a little confusing," Brad said thoughtfully. "It seems like there are different aspects of Trust. I mean it's one thing to not believe someone has the ability to do some task correctly if they've never done it before or if it's a real stretch from their experience. That's something I can work with. But when the issue is more about ethics or morality, it feels very different. Years ago, I worked for a leader who was as polished and slick as you could imagine, but the closer I got to him, the more I saw that a lot of what he was projecting wasn't what his personal life showed. I lost respect for him in a million small ways, even as he was growing the organization with bold projects and huge sales numbers. I wasn't even surprised, just sad, when it came out that he had misused corporate funds and had an affair with his secretary."

It seemed everyone had at least one similar story to share of a leader whose character flaws had destroyed what was otherwise a thriving situation for them. It was a sobering reminder to them all of how quickly everything they had achieved could be ruined.

Stacy had been quiet throughout the conversation, but now she broke her silence. "So if trust depends on both ability and morality, does it increase and decrease for both in the same ways?"

"Not exactly, at least for me," Brad replied. "I've found that people who fail because they lack competence can often recover. In fact, it's usually my fault if I give someone a task they aren't properly prepared for. But if someone fails personally, it's a lot harder to deal with it. Skills can be taught but character doesn't usually change."

"As a pastor I'm kind of in the character-change business, at least in part." Jim joined in, "But I have to agree with you overall. We can work through small issues, but some lines can't be crossed. Even in my world, most leaders who mess up in big ways on the character stuff have to leave the organization. Some of them rebound somewhere else, but sadly a lot don't."

Nina sighed. "This is kind of discouraging. I mean, I agree with everything you're all saying, but it raises the bar pretty high, especially for leaders, and especially when it comes to character."

There was general agreement, and a reflective mood settled in. The group tried to summarize the essentials of what trust meant to them and came up with a rough description that worked: *Trust is confidence in someone's character and competence, that they will give their best and their best will be good enough. A lack of trust creates negative friction that slows progress and undermines both results and relationships.*

The group was feeling pretty good about their conversation until Jim spoke up. "Is any of this actually helpful to you, Stacy? It's all good in theory but you've got a school to run tomorrow, and even the best of platitudes aren't going to do you any good if they don't make a difference in the hallways and classrooms."

"I'm honestly not sure yet. I mean, some of this is just putting words to what we already know. It's common sense. But I'm hoping there's something here that can start to pick the lock."

Prompted by some good questions, Stacy described the situation at Forest Secondary as well as she could understand and explain it. Others made notes as she talked and, after they felt they had reasonable clarity, Neil asked what suggestions they had for her. Together they began to form a plan.

After a focused twenty-five minutes, Stacy reflected back what she had heard and what she thought were the best next steps:

- I need to understand whether the distrust is mostly about competence or character. That will change whether I handle it by training people or confronting them.
- I need to take small steps to build my own credibility with people throughout the school. I can't lead them anywhere if they don't trust me. Both history and temperament make trust really hard for some people to give.
- I need to find some quick wins to start. There are some situations where a little work can show positive results. If I can string a few of those together, it can be the start of momentum.
- I need to face my insecurities. Feeling like this is beyond my ability makes it all harder, and also tempts me to violate my own character standards to try to manipulate the situation. I can take small risks of vulnerability to show that I'm sincere about earning their confidence.
- I need to ask for help. I've been avoiding reaching out to people both within the school and at the board because I want to appear in control, but all this does is keep me from getting better perspective and assistance.
- I need to pay attention to the other aspects of REACTION. Trust is the foundation, but it will help if I can give everyone a glimpse of where we're going and what can be possible if we can begin to pull together.

It was a lot to take on, but they all agreed it was the best approach. More than that, they all offered specific ways they could each lend a hand. Brad was friends with the superintendent and would give her a heads-up that Stacy was going to be asking for some added support. Nina promised to take Stacy out for a run and a chat at least once a week to help clear her head and keep her well-being on track. Amir would check in twice weekly to share more insights from his experience and to debrief the specifics of what Stacy had tried. Neil offered to present the REACTION dashboard at a staff meeting so that the whole team would have to face the elephant in the room in a practical way. Jim promised to clear his schedule by eight every night for the next three weeks, except for a crucial elders' meeting, so he could be home with Stacy to relax and refocus together at the end of the day.

It was a highly engaged group that began to gather their jackets before Neil stopped them.

"This has been really great. Tonight particularly, but really the whole process of digging into REACTION together. I've learned so much from all of you and I feel more confident that this can be helpful. But we've looked at all the elements over the last several sessions and I'm not really sure what to do next. Camp starts in a couple weeks and I'll be fully invested there until September. Where do we go from here?"

No one wanted the group to end, but they acknowledged that Neil was right. They had finished what they had first agreed to do together. Not only had they learned a lot, they had begun to rely on one another for support and insight.

"I have a suggestion," said Brad. "Could we agree to meet up once every three months to check in together, do the dashboard again, and provide each other with feedback? I admit that I wasn't entirely sure what a big-shot corporate guy like me could learn from all of you, but this has become one of the most valuable learning experiences of my career. I'd hate to end it while there's still so much to explore as I try to make REACTION part of my leadership on an ongoing basis."

Everyone agreed and quickly grabbed their phones to set a date for a catch-up and REACTION session each quarter for the next year.

# Chapter Eight – Epilogue

It was a comfortably warm spring evening nine months later as the group, minus one regular member, gathered on Stacy and Jim's back deck for a barbecue and REACTION catch-up. Casual conversation flowed easily with the familiarity that comes among those who have shared the ups and downs of leadership together.

"I'm so sorry Amir can't be with us," Nina said. "It seemed so sudden when he left Hope Springs. We didn't really get a chance to say much more than a quick goodbye."

"He sent me a message this afternoon to share with everybody," Neil said, pulling out his phone.

"*Hello friends, and sadly, farewell. I'm sorry to not be with you tonight and moving forward. I didn't have much time between resigning from Hope Springs and starting my new role out here on the West Coast. Getting loose ends sorted for work and family meant I wasn't able to meet with each of you, as much as I would have liked to. I hope you'll accept this inferior expression of my appreciation for your contributions to my leadership and learning this last year and a half, and a too-short explanation of my decision to move on.*

"*In all of the professional and leadership training I have been privileged to be a part of in my life I don't think I've ever found a more diverse or more helpful group of peers. Your honesty, insight, and vulnerability took the simple REACTION idea and made it something truly formative for how I approach my work. I am truly grateful for how our discussions, both in the group and individually, gave me a deeper understanding and sensitivity towards the importance of culture.*

"*It was actually those discussions that indirectly led to my departure from Hope Springs. This is not public knowledge, but my resignation was not initially motivated by my new opportunity as a mental health advocate and consultant out here. The truth is that*

*I was having a growing disconnect with my board. I had become convinced that, in order to improve our culture, we had to narrow our focus and invest more resources in our people's development, but they were driving a more aggressive growth strategy that would demand all our capacity. To be fair, all of that was explained when I took the job; I was the one who changed. I still believe Hope Springs can continue to increase its scale and impact, but the things you've helped me learn about culture meant I couldn't commit to the pace of growth they wanted. We tried to find middle ground, and perhaps we might have reached a compromise in time, but I really want to spend the next stage of my career exploring this culture concept as deeply as I can. I don't know it well enough yet to pursue it while simultaneously leading that degree of expansion. I know I can trust your discretion to keep this within our small circle.*

"I do hope to stay in touch with each of you and cheer on your work and your lives more fully. Know that you have a friend here who would love to continue the conversations, even if it's at a distance."

Stacy spoke first. "I'm not entirely surprised to hear this. It did seem that Amir was feeling torn between the pressure of the strategic plan and his desire to champion a healthy atmosphere for everyone involved."

"I feel the same thing, even on a smaller scale," Neil added. "I think it must be possible to have a strong culture as well as a commitment to growing my camp and taking on new things, but it feels like there's a natural tension between them sometimes."

There were understanding nods around the table as Nina spoke up: "Sure, there can be tension between strategy and culture in any organization. But they really go hand in hand, don't they? I mean, the strategy drives the culture, or maybe it's the other way around. But we need both."

No one disagreed with Nina's observation, but Stacy felt there was still something missing. "What about doing the actual day-to-day work? I don't know about you all, but I spend most of my day at the school just doing the regular activities of school. Meetings, reports, supervision, and dealing with whatever comes up in the course of the day consumes the bulk of my time. I have to be pretty intentional to pay attention to our big-picture strategy, and a lot of the culture stuff I try to do on the fly in the midst of the busyness of everyday."

"That's definitely the case at Green Leaf," Brad said. "Even the Executive Team have our ongoing grind of work to keep the ship moving. We do strategy updates monthly and dig deeper into it at offsite sessions a couple times a year, but most of my effort is spent executing on the decisions we've made. Adding an emphasis on culture is beginning to show real benefits in my division, to the point where a couple of other VPs have asked me what I'm doing that's changing the tone of my team. It seems like something is added to my workload. Something that helps, though."

For several minutes the conversation flowed around the relationship between culture, strategy, and execution, and more than one of the group wished Amir had been there with his knack for synthesizing the most applicable points of any conversation.

Eventually Jim brought out some notepaper from his office and drew three simple intersecting circles.

"I think it's something like this," he said as he put the page in the middle of the table. "As leaders we have to be on top of Execution all the time. That's what drives the day-to-day reality of the job. But we also have to be able to get that high view where we can see what's on the horizon and where the organization needs to be going and how to get there. That's Strategy. And in the midst of all of that, we are, often unintentionally, setting expectations about the ways all of that stuff is done, the way we interact with and treat each other. That's Culture."

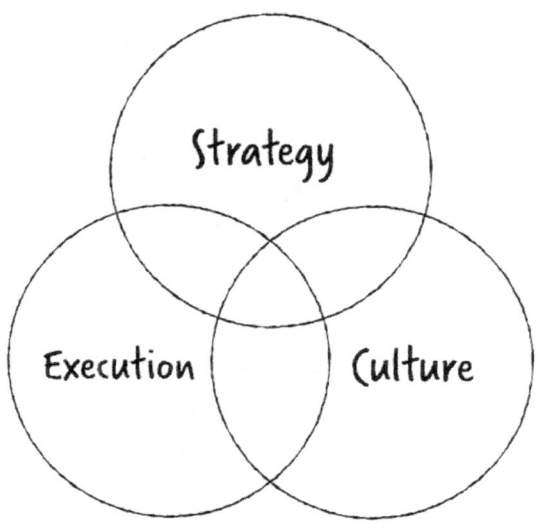

"So which is most important?" Nina asked.

"Can't it be all of them?" Stacy replied. "I mean, as I'm seeing some good results in making things better at Forest, I can point to things we're doing in all of those areas. I work with my department heads and team leads on ideas and projects that impact all three. And, honestly, a lot of the time I don't really consider which of them it is—I just push for what makes the school better."

"And it's working," Neil interjected. "A couple of my camp staff go to Forest and they've noticed the changes. There are some specific things they mention that are better, like the cleaner cafeteria and more extracurricular activities and events, but there's also just a different feel to the whole place."

"You know, Stacy, I think you've been working mostly at Culture. That's what you talk about when you come home." Jim looked from his wife to the picture on the page. "I'm not saying that's the most important necessarily, but you're always telling me about little things you're doing and seeing other people do that help with the culture."

"I guess you're right," Stacy said thoughtfully. "For most of the past year, I really have been digging into the Culture stuff, using REACTION as my mindset. But now that things seem a little better, I find myself drawn more into Strategy, trying to figure out what it will take to hit some specific academic and community targets."

"That makes sense to me," Nina affirmed. "I think as Go Out and Play keeps growing I find I need to really stay on top of Execution. I'm spending more time writing policy and procedure manuals, and doing technical training with new staff than anything else. But I know it's part of the Strategy and that it's the Culture we've built that keeps my clients coming back."

"Maybe the three are all always happening, and we can't ignore any of them for long without serious consequences, but certain situations or seasons benefit from us giving priority to one of them," Brad was thinking out loud. "And maybe a lot of what we do is actually connected to two or three of them at the same time."

**Leaders can never ignore Strategy, Execution, or Culture for long.**

"So it's like Stacy said," Nina added. "With an awareness of all of them, we can do a better job of noticing what we need to be doing to bring out the best in our people right now and in the future."

Agreement was unanimous. As each took a turn to update the others on their work situations, they found themselves using not only the REACTION language, but now also the added vocabulary of Strategy, Execution, and Culture. Time passed quickly, punctuated by both laughter and reflection as they challenged and encouraged one another. Ideas were tested, suggestions made, and resources recommended; this had become such a familiar rhythm that few prompts were needed and no one was really sure anymore if anyone was in charge.

Before they noticed it, the sun was setting and the first bugs of the evening had begun to buzz around, indicating it was probably time to go home.

"Hey Neil," Jim said as they all picked up plates and cups to clear the table. "We've gotten so used to these REACTION conversations that I sometimes forget it all started with you inviting us to hear the basic idea you were developing about a year and a half ago.

"As much as we've all helped add some depth and application to what you shared that night, this was yours to begin with. I really want to thank you for it, and for everything that's come from it for me and Stacy, and for the church and the school. It's making a big difference in how each of us lead, and I know we've got a long way to keep going."

Before Neil could reply both Stacy and Nina added their own affirmations.

Brad, ever the father, couldn't resist teasing his son: "So this REACTION Dashboard is a solid accomplishment. Well done. But haven't you got anything newer to show us?"

The warm laughter paused when Neil thoughtfully said, "Well, I have been doing some thinking. Maybe I can bounce some of those ideas off all of you next time…"

# The Elements

# The Elements – Reason

*"He who has a **why** to live can bear almost any how." – Frederick Nietzsche*
*"To infinity and beyond!" – Buzz Lightyear*

Reason is the answer to the critical question, "Why are we doing this?"

Much more than just a mission statement posted on the wall, Reason is the compelling motivation for everything done within the organization and for your clientele to connect with you at all.

Experientially we know the difference in our approach when we understand and care about the reason for what we're doing and when we don't. A Reason we find compelling draws our attention, effort and loyalty. Reason that is fuzzy or meaningless to us leaves us wanting something more and offering something less.

Reach Forth is a nonprofit that has offered a variety of sports programs for all ages for a couple generations. A few years ago they asked me to volunteer, convening the youth hockey program with more than 300 players. On my way to my first preseason meeting with our forty-plus coaches, I found myself pondering what to tell them beyond the logistics of rosters, schedules, and rules for the year.

A few minutes before we started, I ducked into a side room and jotted a couple of notes that have become the heart of our league and many of the other programs as well.

I told the gathered coaches that we really have just two particular objectives for the season:

1. We are a recreational league.

There are other leagues in our community that offer more ice time, better trained coaches, and a higher focus on skill development. Our players aren't with us to maximize their hockey potential; they are there to have fun. I told our coaches that we can measure the success of this objective by looking for smiles on the faces of the three least talented players on their bench.

2. We want to smell like Jesus.

Strange as that sounds, the idea is rooted in a verse of the Bible that says: "For we are to God the pleasing aroma of Christ among those who are being saved and those who are perishing." (2 Corinthians 2:15). In a sport renowned for stinky equipment bags, this is a fitting reminder that at Reach Forth we aspire to demonstrate the truth and grace of Jesus in everything we do. We can tell this is happening when there are conversations and questions about faith and life mixed in with the game-related banter in the locker rooms and hallways of the arena.

The response from both long-time volunteers and brand new ones has been strongly positive. Each year since then we return to these two objectives repeatedly, highlighting examples of them being done well, and challenging ourselves when we fall short. A few people have decided this isn't what they're looking for—and we can graciously help them find another place to play. It's been satisfying for me to see that these basics of Reason have continued in Reach Forth in the years since my own involvement has come to an end.

Having to remind all our stakeholders frequently of our Reason and seeing some decide to opt out because of it demonstrates key understandings about Reason.

Reason done right connects with us in two distinct ways.

*First, we have to understand it.* As obvious as this may appear, it isn't always the case. Ensuring that the Reason is defined and communicated frequently and in a variety of ways is the first responsibility of leaders in developing or strengthening organizational culture.

When founding a new organization, it may seem that the Reason is quite obvious, but it may not be. Many founders get by on energy and enthusiasm, drawing people into a vague dream with their personal charisma but not much defined substance. Getting Reason right requires slowing down enough to really dig in and consider the needs, opportunities, and strengths available.

Established organizations can also struggle. In many cases Reason was never carefully defined in the first place, and in many others, the original Reason may need to be clarified, revised, or improved upon. Circumstances change in the surrounding community and culture, and Reason must adapt to remain relevant. When this happens without intent we call it "mission drift" and it is something to avoid. But when we recognize the need to adjust our Reason and do it deliberately, it can become an important milepost in the story of the organization.

*Secondly, we have to care about it.* If the Reason doesn't connect with my values and priorities, it will never win my best efforts. People don't all care about the same things, so a strong Reason becomes an effective filter for finding those who "get it" and those who don't. A truly worthwhile Reason will at times require more than a casual following along; it will call people to personal involvement that only those who truly care will be inclined to give.

**Reason that doesn't connect with my values and priorities will never win my best efforts.**

Caring is no substitute for the ability to actually get the job done, and demanding blind allegiance and sacrifice from every fringe member of the organization is more likely a sign of an unhealthy organization than a healthy one, but people who don't sincerely care about the Reason will eventually pull the whole organization toward mediocrity. It takes courage and conviction to call people to a Reason worth caring about.

This is why when we score Reason on the REACTION Dashboard we combine the ideas of knowing and caring. It has to be both to bring out our best and inspire others to join in.

It is the responsibility of leadership to ensure that the Reason is defined and communicated well enough that all the stakeholders can understand it. It almost always takes more time than expected because we discover that there are differences of opinion even within the leadership circle on exactly why we exist as an organization.

Once we understand it, we must communicate it. The challenge here is to communicate it with enough frequency and variety to ensure that everyone can understand and those who care are able to engage.

**5 S's of Communicating Reason**

Current education theory shows us that people learn in different ways. Communicating Reason then must be done in multiple forms if we really want people to be able to grasp it. I recommend leaders learn to use 5 S's to communicate Reason.

Slogan: Most organizations do a decent job of coming up with a brief catch-phrase or sentence to express their Reason. These may be seasonal, focused on a particular emphasis or project, or more lasting with relevance to the real why of the entire operation. A well-crafted slogan is short enough to fit on a T-shirt or a tweet. It either gives enough information to answer the why question, or raises enough curiosity to have those who read it make the effort to contact you for the answer.

Story: Brain science tells us that stories unlock neurological patterns of empathy, drawing us into connection with the characters in the story and those telling it. Too often we leave storytelling in the realm of marketing alone when it belongs in every aspect of your leadership. It should be a required skill that everyone in your organization can tell at least one engaging story that expresses the Reason for your organization. When I served as board chair at one charity, we began every meeting with a story from the frontlines about the needs we faced and how we were making a difference. It set a tone of relevance and importance for our conversations.

Statistics: Numbers have authority. They speak to the scale of the problem you are addressing or the degree to which your solutions are working. It is essential that your statistics are accurate and fully supportable because critics and competitors will expose sloppy analytics. It is better to know a few statistics confidently, and to be prepared to get other numbers later than to risk being found to have exaggerated or misinterpreted them. Every leader should have a couple of relevant and credible statistics ready to share. They don't need to be minutely detailed; they just need to demonstrate the importance of what you are doing.

Symbol: In an increasingly visual society a well-designed image is a powerful communications tool. Whether it be a logo, campaign poster, infographic, or internet meme; a picture is often worth far more than a thousand words. A visual icon of some type can explain and remind both internal and external audiences of your Reason. Hiring or contracting skilled graphics people is becoming a necessity, even in smaller organizations. What's important is how the symbol is perceived by the people you want to reach, not whether it suits your personal preferences.

Strategy: Once people have begun to grasp the need for what you do, they will want to know how you are going to accomplish it. A brief summary of your strategy, that is simplified but not simplistic, answers the most anticipated questions before they are asked. Being able to articulate a well-thought-out strategy builds confidence that you are the right ones to take on the challenges you are seeking to address. It may well be that your audience doesn't have the time or expertise to grasp every aspect of your model, but they do want to know that you know what you're doing. A one-page document, a two-minute video, or a short conversation will be enough to satisfy most people. Save the detail for those who are ready to dig deeper.

**Reason Leaks**

During the many summers I spent working at camps, one of the oft-repeated phrases was "Camp is for the campers." It was a reminder to me as a teenaged leader that as much as I was enjoying the staff-only volleyball game, if there were children sitting bored by the side of the court, we needed to invite them to play. I didn't always appreciate that. At times I joined my fellow counsellors in mocking the phrase and rolling my eyes when it was mentioned, but it echoes in my mind even a couple decades later.

The camp directors and senior staff surely knew how we reacted to the well-worn slogan, but they also knew that we needed to hear it. It wasn't enough to go over it once during staff training week at the end of June. It had to be repeated throughout the summer.

Reason leaks.

We need to reinvigorate Reason frequently. When I say Reason leaks, I mean that it easily and naturally gets reduced, watered down, or neglected with all the competing priorities and interests we have. Even a fascinating and compelling Reason is vulnerable to becoming diluted.

The only solution is to continually bring it back to the foreground of our minds by repeating it, sometimes in different forms or words, and more often than we think should be necessary.

Leaders are often concerned that repeating the Reason frequently is going to be a waste of time and will be perceived as insulting to their people. This is almost never the case. The truth is that in most cases leaders are not repeating the Reason nearly enough.

Admittedly, simply chanting a slogan from memory at the beginning of every day may lose impact over time. Instead, skilled leaders utilize all 5 S's and are attuned for spontaneous opportunities to reinforce the Reason as they occur. They also make a point of having regular reminders scheduled so they too don't risk forgetting.

When I worked as a pastor, I was hired by a church that served communion every Sunday, while churches I had previously been involved in served it monthly or less. It was remarkable how knowing that communion was part of the service impacted my sermons. I knew I had to tie whatever I was speaking on into the core Reason for Christianity: the story and sacrifice of Jesus. This prevented me from getting lost in general self-help ideas or academic speculation. Every Sunday we were returning to our Reason.

The challenge in returning to our Reason so often was to continue to explore the deep meaning of what could have become an empty ritual. It was enlivening and at times challenging to be compelled to recognize all the ways that the simple bread and wine (or grape juice) and a familiar 2000-year-old story could have resonance and relevance for our community week by week.

There are people who may find the frequent reinforcement of Reason annoying, just as I did when I worked at camps. Wise leaders will consider whether this is an issue of the Reason being repeated without meaning or creativity, or whether it is just that the individuals don't understand or care about it.

If proper attention is taken to ensure that the Reason is understood and some creativity is used in reinforcing it through all 5 S's, then those who are significantly bothered by the repetition are most likely not truly a fit for the organization. It is probably time for an honest conversation about their continued involvement.

<u>Individual Reason</u>

Leaders have primary responsibility for establishing and reinforcing Reason. While you may not be the one who first determined the purpose for the organization, it is now entrusted to you. Generally, leaders should have little trouble understanding the Reason. If it is not properly defined, it must become a top priority to gather the relevant people together and to do the work of defining or refining it.

When Reason is understood we must ask if we actually care. I have great admiration for leaders who have the integrity to acknowledge that they no longer fit an organization because they don't find the Reason compelling. Stepping away to find something more in tune with personal values and aspirations is honourable.

If your own Reason score is lower than you want it to be, it is time for you to consider carefully what you need to do to ensure that the Reason is understood and that you care about it.

<u>Organization Reason</u>

In any organization, there will be a range of responses to each of the REACT factors. When it comes to Reason, leadership should be able to ensure that it is understood by everyone involved in the organization. Proper orientation of new people, regular reinforcement, and use of all 5 S's should keep the understanding aspect of Reason fairly high even during times of refining it.

Concerning scores in this space indicate that either the Reason is not being properly reinforced within the organization, or that members of the team don't care enough about it. Leaders should first revisit the Reason and re-communicate it to all in as many ways as it takes to be confident that it is understood. When that is done, it is time for each person to consider whether they care enough to continue their involvement. A compelling and well-defined Reason can make these hard conversations more clear, if not easier.

In the times of difficulty that come for every organization, the commitment to the Reason is tested. These are opportunities for leaders to recommit themselves to the cause, and to invite others to carefully reflect on their ability to do the same. Persevering through a season of struggle requires caring deeply about a Reason that is clearly understood.

If there are Warning Lights here, it is a useful and insightful exercise to take the time to determine what level of caring is necessary for each role within the organization, based on the degree of commitment required by the Reason. It may be that some roles require only a general agreement with or commitment to the Reason, but those who work on the front lines or represent the organization to outsiders need to buy in.

Network Reason

Defining who is part of your Network can be complex, but recognizing their degree of understanding and caring about your Reason usually isn't. If your Reason is well-defined and relevant, people will be eager to interact with your organization, seeking you out and eagerly engaging. Conversations have a sense of "You too? This is awesome!" happening. Heads nod, smiles broaden, and opportunities sprout like wildflowers.

A weakly understood Reason brings awkward interactions where members of the Network aren't sure what you're really about, or they are sure but they are incorrect. A poorly conceived brand or communication that doesn't properly consider the audience brings wasteful confusion and frustration for everyone involved.

No organization can scale beyond the degree to which their Reason is understood and cared about. Educating and engaging the Network using all 5 S's can increase both aspects, ultimately extending your reach and impact.

# The Elements – Energy

"Energy and persistence conquer all things" – Benjamin Franklin
"The average person puts only 25% of his energy and ability into his work. The world takes off its hat to those put in more than 50% of their capacity, and stands on its head for those few and far between souls who devote 100%" – Andrew Carnegie

High school physics tells us that energy is the capacity to do work. Effective leadership musters as much Energy as possible and directs it in the most effective way towards the Reason.

And yet, report after report affirms that the vast majority of people are disengaged, unmotivated, and giving far less than their best to their work. This is not just a frustration; it's a tragic waste. And it is as discouraging to workers who long to be part of something that inspires their best efforts as it is to leaders who would love to tap into all that potential.

This Energy crisis has two fronts. First many of us simply don't have all that much energy to offer to any aspect of our lives. Second, our work often gets the least amount of energy possible.

Leaders tend to be high-energy people. But that doesn't mean there isn't plenty of room to increase our energy stores. Basic changes in our health; appropriate nutrition, regular exercise, and particularly getting a reasonable amount of sleep can contribute to having a significantly larger energy capacity. If your Individual energy is a concern, a conversation with your family doctor is a great place to start. There may be underlying medical issues at play. There are many good resources for those who want to become healthier and more physically fit. Suffice it to say that most of us could make a significant improvement by simply doing the things we already know we should be doing.

Beyond the physical limits of health and fitness, energy levels are also dependent on a variety of psychological factors. Almost any one of the multitude of personality assessment tools available can be helpful in understanding the kinds of activities and interactions that drain and restore our energy. Using such an assessment as a team provides both insight and a common vocabulary for understanding and discussing how to make the best use of each individual's energy.

Even without engaging a formal tool, leaders can simply list the activities and relationships in their lives that drain them and the ones that energize them. Distinguishing our "get to" work from our "have to" work can be surprisingly insightful.

Awareness of how we are energized can also have profound relevance for our planning. For years we have been trained on how to make the most of our time, and most leaders know these principles, although applying them is another thing altogether. What we may not understand is how to manage our energy.

It is unrealistic to expect our energy levels to remain high at all times. We are biologically and psychologically, not to mention spiritually, wired for cycles of building and depleting energy.

**We are wired for cycles of building and depleting energy.**

Learning to use these cycles strategically can make us more effective in the short term while also increasing our energy capacity for future needs. Interspersing energizing activities among draining ones, timing critical tasks for times when we are typically full of energy, and watching for patterns of times of diminished energy can all increase both our productivity and our enthusiasm for what we do.

We can also build our understanding of the natural fluctuations in energy that happen throughout the day, week, month, or year. These patterns become valuable in determining how and when to schedule intentional blocks of recuperation when we can anticipate being worn out, and in anticipation of times of higher demand. We can resist the tendency to pile draining events closely together and make a point to balance them with activities that are rejuvenating.

Just as we apply knowledge of energy capacity and cycles to

ourselves, they are equally relevant in our organizations. Effective leaders will learn the best ways to energize their team members, and to note those things that regularly drain them. They will be particularly alert for the droop that predictably follows times of high demand, and will make a point of providing opportunity for invigorating or restful activities before people are on empty.

Of course, energy is affected by life outside of work as well. We like to behave as if we had separate energy tanks for each area of our lives—work, family, faith, hobbies, friends, exercise, volunteering—but of course we don't. We do have the freedom to allocate whatever energy we have to any of those areas, but always at the expense of the others. Energy demands in one area of life reduce what is available for other areas.

This raises the idea of trying to find balance, developing a system where each aspect of life receives a stable, consistent amount of energy that ensures that we can accomplish everything we desire. Sadly, that kind of balance is a myth.

In real life, balance is more like riding a bicycle. A bike is pretty much never in balance. Riders are continually making tiny, unconscious adjustments from one side to the other, constantly correcting and re-correcting to keep themselves from tipping over. Only the most skilled and practiced cyclists can balance a bike in one spot for more than a few seconds.

Likewise, we continually manage demands on our energy (and time for that matter) that pull us out of balance. Rather than trying to figure out a perfect equation for stability, we would do well to accept that we will never have everything perfect and instead to make adjustments to accommodate the inconsistent, unscheduled, and often inconvenient realities of life.

And just as a bicycle balances best when it is moving, it is easiest to manage our energy when we know where we want to be going.

<u>Individual Energy</u>

Most leaders have higher-than-average energy. It's a big part of what allows leaders to accomplish all that they so often do. However, that doesn't come with invulnerability to Energy issues.

If your energy score is a concern, start by considering the overall energy demands of your life. It may be that you are just in a particularly draining season that is likely to pass in a reasonably short time. It may be that there is really little to be done other than to reduce your expectations of yourself, buckle down, and get through the challenges of the moment.

More frequently, our energy concerns reflect an ongoing issue that is some combination of two factors: not having enough energy in our tank to begin with; and, not using our energy well.

To increase our effectiveness, we need to become expert in our own energy levels. This starts with understanding where our energy comes from. Beyond basic health and fitness, we all have people, activities, and habits that drain us and others that fuel us. Very few people can ever hope to be able to eliminate all the draining tasks from our lives, but we can be intentional about not allowing too many draining activities to happen in succession to the point where we are worn out.

Using time off well is an underrated skill. The best leaders I know all have significant interests outside of work. Some are artists and musicians, others are talented home chefs or gardeners, and many are athletes. The majority are involved as volunteers in their community in some way, whether it be coaching youth sports, serving on a charity's board of directors, or participating actively in their spiritual community.

The same leadership skills that are effective in the workplace are often displayed in a refreshing way in these contexts. At other times it is precisely a break from leadership responsibilities that makes off time truly a form of re-creation, providing the rest and change of perspective that prepares leaders to step back into their work ready to engage.

**Self-Care and Stress Strategies**

Managing personal energy requires developing attentiveness to both how we increase our baseline energy level and how we respond under stress.

Most of us are well aware of the fundamental need for proper nutrition and exercise. The best leaders I know are active people who take their health seriously. Some are rigidly disciplined, but others have a more spontaneous approach. Either can work so long as it leads to consistently eating well and exercising.

Too many leaders, on the other hand, neglect rest and sleep. Driven to accomplish important things, we easily fall into habits of insufficient recovery, sustaining our efforts with caffeine and sugar. (This is one of my own problem areas.) We know that the average adult requires eight hours of sleep each night to perform well, but we credit ourselves with being beyond average and get by on significantly less. The effects on our mood, relationships, decision-making, and long-term success are ignored for as long as possible.

Particularly during times of increased stress, healthy leaders prioritize three strategies to maintain their wellness:

1. Safe People – Healthy leaders spend time with trustworthy friends, clergy, or counsellors who will "speak the truth with love," neither flattering nor bullying us. These "safe but not soft" (to use the wonderful phrase from Arrow Leadership) people help us to remember what is truly important and to regain our centre.
2. Soothing Practices – Healthy leaders take time to do the things that comfort us at a deeper level. These may be spiritual habits, time in nature, exercise, art, or even indulging in some mindless entertainment. The purpose is to rest our minds and nurture our souls.
3. Still Places – We need peace and quiet. Whether it is a park, a library, a few extra moments alone in the car, or a more intentionally designed place of sanctuary in our homes or elsewhere, we need to identify and experience periods of stillness and solitude to be prepared for the often hectic reality of daily leadership.

Leaders who make a point of building their energy on a continual basis and recognize their need for breaks from the stress set a worthy example for their teams and equip themselves for lasting influence.

<u>Organization Energy</u>

Leaders wanting to address concerns regarding Organizational Energy need to keep in mind that every organization is, of course, made up of individuals. Each person's energy level has an impact on the overall energy level; and low-energy people tend to drag the whole group down.

An organization that wants to address energy concerns has to consider whether the issue is rooted in people not having enough energy at all, or in them not bringing enough of it to work. Energy truly is a holistic matter. No organization can thrive when its people are drained; and no organization can control the influences beyond the work environment that may be either energizing or draining.

While it has become a trendy perk for companies to offer gym memberships, running clubs, yoga classes or even treadmill-equipped meeting rooms, these are merely attempts to develop a culture in which employees have greater health and more energy available for work. The value of these strategies is debatable, but the intent is wise. People who eat well, rest well, and are active will have fewer sick days and generally better emotional states, and will be equipped to offer more energy to every area of their lives.

Leaders can recognize when work demands are particularly high for their team, and choose to schedule periods of relative recovery to prepare for or to follow draining events, projects, or seasons. We can also be sensitive to the realities of life beyond work for our people. If work always functions as an energy drain, it will breed resentment as family, community involvement, recreation, and rest have to draw on limited leftovers.

This is even more complicated when employees are so committed to the Reason that they fail to manage their own energy well. Passion for the cause can become a detriment when it leads to extended strain in other areas of life. A healthy organization takes a long-term approach to energy, which may mean training eager staff to slow down a little and be attentive to their health, interests, and relationships.

We are just beginning to break the societal obsession with being busy. Despite solid medical evidence and endless anecdotal support, there is still a perception that working harder, doing more, and giving some mathematically impossible 110% is a mark of good leadership. It remains too rare to find a leader who maintains a reasonable margin in life. This unhealthy pattern then becomes the default expectation for everyone else.

Using the REACTION tool with organizations has repeatedly revealed leaders who have seemingly inhuman energy capacity. Their teams truly regard them as anomalies in the sheer volume of things they can accomplish, and the minimal amounts of rest and recovery they need to sustain their efforts. This is a great resource to the leader but can hurt the organization when others perceive some pressure (real or imagined) to match that productivity. As in many other areas, leaders set the tone.

Sometimes leaders need to deliberately challenge or change the idea that their example is the expectation for everyone in the organization. It's not enough to just say it; they may need to change their patterns to create space for others to work sustainably. Avoiding sending late night emails, leaving the office at the end of the typical workday (even if they return later for a couple hours), or taking a couple days off after major deadlines or extended work travel can communicate that others are free to do the same.

<u>Network Energy</u>

By definition, the Network is outside the Organization, so the effect any leader can have on the disparate components of the Network is limited. There are, however, at least two key insights that can gained from Network Energy that are strategically valuable.

First, be aware of the Energy level of the Network. A depleted system has little to give to you, no matter how wonderful your offerings may be. Sometimes brilliant initiatives fail simply because the people you want to reach don't have the capacity to engage.

The simplest example of this reality is in finances. Money is a form of energy, and corporations, start-ups, and charities are all too well aware of how external factors limit the ability of even the highly committed to contribute. The repeated financial turmoil of recent years has left many worthy projects and causes unfunded. Some wise leaders have recognized this situation, delaying or reducing key campaigns because the Network just couldn't come up with the required resources.

The same is true of other forms of energy. People who are distracted, tired, or burned out can't participate in the same way that energized people can. Capitalizing on periods of opportunity when people are able to respond is a critical skill.

It may even be that your organization is able to help your Network increase their Energy. Encouraging best practices, providing tank-filling opportunities, and setting a healthy example may enable others to extend their capacity, and that can only help when you invite them to use their precious Energy towards your Reason.

The second critical insight is this: Understand how your Network decide how to allocate their Energy. These choices are made continuously, and often subconsciously. Even the process of making a choice requires energy, so drained Networks tend to keep doing the same things until something forces a choice to change.

Taking the time to ask how your most engaged partners make the decisions to be involved with you can provide great ideas for attracting more from others. And finding out why others don't engage with you is at least equally insightful.

Some leaders have discovered that their Network responds to an uncommonly high Energy demand. Their constituents embrace commitment and challenge. They like the sense of giving more than others do, and they expect that level of Energy to be reciprocated. Others have learned that lowering the bar to entry can bring a significant response from a Network that wants to get involved but can't meet the real or perceived minimum threshold. Providing a less demanding option can open up opportunities.

A leader who becomes a student of managing Energy can discover and release surprising possibilities as an Individual, within their organization, and often extending into their network.

# The Elements – Alignment

"Alignment is a demonstration of humility, submitting to the vision and strategy." – Andy Crouch
"Tell all the fish to swim down" – Nemo

Near the end of the Disney movie Finding Nemo, there's a scene that captures the idea of Alignment perfectly. You might remember it.

The little clown fish, Nemo, and his father have finally been reunited when suddenly their friend Dory is captured in the net of a trawler with what appear to be hundreds of other fish. As they begin to be hauled toward the surface with the fish swimming wildly in search of an escape, Nemo bravely swims into the net. He calls on all the fish to "swim down" and, with his father and Dory joining in the encouragement, the fish begin to orient themselves vertically. Just when it appears all is lost, the combined power of all the fish moving in the same direction overwhelms the winch on the boat. The trawler arm breaks, the net falls loose, and the fish are dramatically rescued by Nemo's leadership and their united effort.

It's amazing what can happen when we use all our Energy in the same direction. Alignment means applying all the combined Energy towards the Reason.

In theory it should be fairly simple to stay aligned. Once the Reason is properly delineated all we have to do is stay focused on the important stuff and refuse to be distracted. Simple, right?

Reality is much more challenging.

A leader's typical day involves a swirling mix of meetings, research, responding to email, checking in on people and projects, and trying to keep all the balls she's juggling from crashing around her and landing on everyone else. With so much going on it can be hard to even remember the Reason at all, let alone assure that every bit of our Energy, and that of everyone else, is being applied correctly. That demanding churn is unrelenting, which is why it's so crucial for leaders to check the Dashboard occasionally to consider their Alignment.

A quick assessment of the percentage of time (which is often easier to consider than Energy) spent on actual productive work is a start. Using a timeframe of at least a week or at most a month seems to provide enough data to be useful while still manageable. Rough estimates are all that's needed initially. A full workflow analysis may be appropriate at some point but that is a demanding task that may not be entirely worthwhile.

Listing the tasks that demand the most energy, and determining to what degree they are actually relevant to the Reason can be eye-opening, and occasionally discouraging. Leadership does typically require involvement in a variety of duties that may not appear closely connected to key results. Responses to this understanding can vary between two extremes.

Some leaders see everything they do as relevant to Reason. They can make an argument that their entire calendar is mission-critical, usually appealing to tangential connections that require some mental gymnastics to appreciate. This is usually a sign of either selfish arrogance or poor accountability. These leaders have over-identified their own role with the organization's purpose. Establishing a focused Reason and effective reporting make a big difference.

Other leaders feel like nothing they do is actually relevant. They find themselves chasing the day, responding to every stimulus and demand, unable to take control and to do what matters most. This demonstrates a combination of poor systems and lack of discipline. There are numerous tools and resources to help focus on priorities. It often takes experimenting with several approaches to find what works best for any individual. Investing a little time and money can enable even easily distracted leaders to get things done.

**Searchlight, Spotlight, Laser**

Contrary to what some might believe, the best leaders are not

100% focused 100% of the time. Not only would that be obsessive, it wouldn't get best results.

Few leaders have roles so narrow and repetitive that they can lock in their focus the same way all the time. We need to spread our energy to understand our entire industry and the many external factors that impact it. We also have to be able to give attention to particular needs and opportunities that appear relevant. And, finally, we need to be able to take on specific situations with intensity.

Using the images of a Searchlight, Spotlight, and Laser provides a framework to do all of these things as they are needed.

Searchlight: Leaders are Learners. In most cases this means there are aspects of our roles in which we are generalists rather than technical experts. We need to have a broad understanding of the diverse factors that affect our work, and what is happening beyond our specific operations.

Like a moving light searching the skies for incoming planes during World War II, we need to scan the horizon for things that could be relevant. Reading newspapers and trade journals, attending conferences, and even scanning social media can introduce us to people, ideas, and resources that may prove helpful. A browsing approach, rather than deliberate research, opens us to possibilities we might typically miss.

Spotlight: When the Searchlight illuminates something intriguing, or we have a sense of what we are looking for, our approach needs to change. Instead of scanning widely, we want to pay attention and see something in particular.

Several years ago my wife and I saw a professional theatre production of The Lion King. It was amazing! In the darkened theatre we would be watching a singer on one side of the stage when suddenly a spotlight would shine on something moving up the opposite aisle and we would turn to see a remarkable contraption of people, mechanics, and colour that was somehow easily recognized as a giraffe. The spotlight drew our attention to something we really wanted to see.

Whether it be the result of our Searchlight or a targeted search that leads us to something relevant, shining a Spotlight on a book, expert, TED talk, course, or connection helps us assess the value, accuracy, and usefulness it may have.

Laser: When light energy is brought into narrow focus, it can be immensely powerful. We can measure the speed of a fastball, do micro-surgery, and (according to the movies) even blast a threatening asteroid to smithereens before it destroy the Earth. That's the power of the laser.

When it is time to take action, leaders, teams, and organizations that want to have the most impact do so with focused power. The Searchlight and Spotlight have helped us determine exactly how to apply Energy to get the results we want, and we are ready to act decisively.

Dedicating attention, effort and resources to the most impactful areas and the most promising opportunities is laser focus. Effective leaders have a remarkable ability to ignore distractions, identify what is truly important, and devote themselves to what will bring the greatest results.

Every leader needs to become adept in using all three lights, but there is no magical ratio for how much to use each one. In some seasons and circumstances each of them takes priority, and the priorities are continually shifting. Identifying how important each is for what is happening right now and what can be anticipated down the road helps leaders apply Energy effectively.

We also need to understand our innate preferences. Some people tend to focus excessively on Searchlight behaviour and need to remember that endless browsing and broad knowledge alone doesn't get results. Others love to research and build detailed plans and models, far beyond the needs of the situation. And many leaders have such a bias for action that they fail to ever look around to see what else is happening.

Using the Searchlight, Spotlight, Laser approach to setting your calendar and your reporting helps ensure that Energy is being applied to Reason in the ways that will best for lasting impact.

**Alignment to Values**

Another area requiring Alignment is organizational values. More will be said about values in the Trust chapter, but for now it should be mentioned that it is not enough to apply all of our Energy to the Reason if we do so in a way that undermines the health of the organization.

There are fundamental aspects of relational decency that should be easily to apparent to everyone—respect, compassion, honesty, and the absence of bullying, abuse, or bigotry, for example. But as our culture seems to be increasingly accepting dismissive and insulting language and behaviour, it may sadly be necessary to remind ourselves of the most basic concepts of The Golden Rule: Treat others the way you would like others to treat you.

Beyond this, each organization has values that define and describe the particular ways they expect people to treat one another and make decisions.

Organizations may differ in terms of values like their preferred degree of formality in communications or clothing, their shared approach to risk, the hours they work, their acceptable expression of conflict, and the way authority is respected and expressed, etc. Being explicit about these cultural-informing values is good leadership and well worth the time involved.

As in explaining our Reason, stories are a high-traction way to share values. My preferred way of identifying these values is to gather the entire team together and to ask them to share stories of the organization when it is at its very best. Not only are these stories part of the positive mythology of the organization, but those who are listening can note the themes that emerge as common across many stories.

Rather than staring at a blank whiteboard and brainstorming a bland, generic list of values that apply everywhere (Excellence! Integrity! Service!), these stories draw attention to the specific things that are true in our organization that might not be the case everywhere else.

**Stories draw attention to the values that are true in our organization.**

I know a small suburban church that was meeting in a school gymnasium while saving money to purchase their own building. At a key moment in their young history, they chose to donate a large portion of their savings to an inner-city congregation that included many people who dealt with addiction and mental illness, experienced homelessness, or survived as sex workers, so that that inner-city congregation could buy their own church building. That demonstrated the first church's value of generosity more powerfully than any facilitated session with a paid consultant could hope to.

By the time we've heard many of the best case stories, there are usually some clear patterns of the behaviours that show "us at our most us." It doesn't take long to translate these into core values.

The next challenge is to hold one another accountable to them.

Healthy cultures aren't ones where no one ever violates the values. (If no one ever steps out of line it's likely that the standard is too low). Instead, they are the ones where those violations are identified quickly and clearly, and where those who have transgressed are called out on their behaviour and called back into the community.

Alignment with values is at least as important as alignment with Reason, and in fact is probably more important.

In either case, the challenge is to be continually reminded of what we are striving for and why it is so significant. Alignment is the way we make the most of our Energy.

# The Elements – Clarity

"The single biggest problem in communication is the illusion that it has taken place."
– George Bernard Shaw
"Comparison is the mother of all clarity." – Os Guinness

Warren was one of my first bosses when I worked at day camps as a teenager, and he gave me a tip that has proven profoundly insightful.

When reviewing my job description, he told me to take particular note of the final line: "Other duties as assigned." Alongside the regular tasks of taking attendance, planning games and crafts, keeping campers safe, and tidying up at the end of the day, there would be some surprises in store during our ten-week summer season.

Over the several years I worked for Warren those "other duties as assigned" included: filling garbage bags with popcorn at a local video store for movie watching on a rainy afternoon; advising and driving home a staff member whose behaviour put him on the edge of being fired; talking to concerned community members; attending a regional conference of recreation leaders; and delivering an impressive quantity of sunscreen to parks all over town. None of those were articulated anywhere on my job description, but they became some of my most memorable days and best leadership lessons.

Warren was right. "Other duties as assigned" was a key part of my role.

With Clarity what we're trying to do is communicate expectations, not just in a top-down, autocratic way, but with a mutuality that allows everyone to know what their job is, how it fits into the bigger picture, and how responsibility, resources, and information flow both to and from them.

Our default strategy for Clarity is the job description, but as in my day-camp days, we often find them incomplete for the variety of tasks and situations that emerge in a particular role over time. And job descriptions are rarely updated as frequently as they should be.

Author Brian Reynolds deserves more recognition for his book "<u>What do you expect?</u>" In it he builds our understanding that responsibilities are too often assumed rather than explicitly stated. Clarity at its best is explicit, mutually agreed-upon expectations. A lack of clarity shows up in confusion, finger-pointing, and things slipping through the cracks. It leads not only to inefficiency, but to accusation, defensiveness, errors, and lost opportunities. Whenever someone says, "I thought you were doing that," the issue is clarity.

Clarity is also often the real issue when someone is overstepping their role. Employees and volunteers who seem to be acting beyond their authority may be difficult people who are trying to build their own kingdoms within your organization, or they may simply be people who truly care about your Reason and want to contribute as much as they can. Their admirable sense of ownership is being frustrated by the sense that what they are doing isn't enough. Re-clarifying how their role is integral to what the organization accomplishes may satisfy their desire for impact.

Clarity's power is that it drives accountability. When expectations are well-communicated and committed to, holding people responsible for their work becomes natural and obvious.

**Clarity's power is that it drives accountability.**

The first performance review I received when I worked as a youth pastor was nerve-wracking. I remember walking into the home of one of our board members to meet with him and the pastor. They presented me with feedback from the ten elders, but with no unified voice. Some of the comments directly contradicted others, and some seemed unrelated to my understanding of my role at all. I was told they wanted to give me a sense of the variety of viewpoints about my work, but instead I left very confused. I had no idea what was most important or what I was supposed to improve.

I wish I'd had the confidence and maturity to ask them to go back and prepare a review with the clarity of a united perspective. It would have helped all of us. In the years that followed, these same leaders gave me remarkable support and increasing clarity in roles that were vulnerable to a lot of confusion.

When Clarity is done well, performance reviews hold no surprises. There is little uncertainty or debate, just affirmation of what is being accomplished and the ability to address inadequacies openly.

<u>Individual Clarity</u>

If you aren't sure of what is expected of you, you're probably in trouble. And if you are sure, but your superiors, peers, or subordinates don't have the same expectations, you are in even more trouble because you don't know it!

Some leaders hesitate to push for Clarity because it feels restrictive or too formal. In fact, doing the hard work of achieving Clarity really functions like the string of a kite, anchoring the situation so it can properly fly. Another analogy some find helpful is that Clarity is like the lines surrounding a sports field. Clarity marks out the specific area in which there is freedom to play.

The process of defining and agreeing to expectations can be uncomfortable, particularly for those who prefer to avoid conflict. But clarity prevents bigger conflict later. It is far easier to push for clarity before something goes significantly wrong and you need to backtrack, apologize, or clean up a mess. The time and energy required up front will pay off with efficiency and effectiveness down the road. And regular updates should be a habit.

I tell leaders that their job description is simple: Make everything awesome!. Of course that's not enough. Clarity determines priorities, and helps us know when to say no. For many leaders, identifying which opportunities to reject is far more helpful than telling them which things to pursue. Regular updates according to established objectives and targets are far more useful than a job description that may be years out of date.

### Organizational Clarity

Role descriptions and workflow charts are useful tools provided they are revised consistently when circumstances change. The problem is that change happens so frequently in many organizations that the time and effort required to update them is a barrier.

Instead of constantly revising, there are less demanding practices that can keep things moving until the scale of change drives a fuller update.

Make a habit of taking a few minutes at the end of every meeting to restate what responsibilities each person is taking with them. You'll likely be surprised how often this reveals gaps or assumptions that aren't shared. Organizations that consistently pause, even when everyone is eager to get the meeting over with, to review precisely what has been committed and by whom have fewer dropped balls and internal squabbles.

When something falls through the cracks, use it as an opportunity to improve and reinforce clarity. Identify how the system/people/process failed to get the desired result and determine whether this was truly an understandable exception or if there is something to be done to prevent a recurrence.

Personality profile tools can be helpful in building an understanding of the degree of detail required by different people to believe they have Clarity. It's not the same for everyone. What feels inadequate and fuzzy for one person may feel stifling to another. Wise leaders strive to provide each person with the clarity they need to do their best work, ensuring that there is no confusion on matters deemed essential.

In addition to workflow expectations, we are in a time where character and moral matters are increasingly in need of Clarity. A continuous stream of scandals reveals that organizations are often held responsible for the behaviour of their leaders in the court of public opinion and in the marketplace. Ethics clauses or codes of conduct are more and more relevant, and professional legal counsel should be part of the drafting and implementation of such documents.

For faith-based organizations this is even more significant. Expectations that were commonly assumed just a generation ago are now being challenged both in court and in the media. Statements of faith and community covenants must be carefully crafted, diligently communicated, and consistently applied. Even then, consideration of revisions to these sometimes controversial documents should be a regular part of governance and leadership.

Any code of conduct reflects the minimum standards of behaviour, whereas a statement of values can point to ideals and best practices. Leaders are often tempted to try to craft a code of conduct that delineates every conceivable ethical situation and prescribes expectations. This is doomed to fail. The pace of change and complexity of real life guarantee that something will be missed or a new dilemma will arise that isn't covered. A healthy culture usually focuses on value statements that build understanding and invite discussion about areas of uncertainty rather than creating a checklist of unacceptable behaviours that may leave people looking for loopholes.

<u>Network Clarity</u>

In many cases Clarity with the Network has long been the most easily applied area. Contracts, memoranda of understanding, agency agreements, and the like are fundamental. We have understood that the differing interests and priorities among the network require explicit agreements.

Following industry best practices for these documents is basic. What is more difficult is ensuring that they remain current as situations and personnel change. Too often network relationships are tied to particular individuals who develop their own shorthand, system, and assumptions for how things are done. When transitions occur, this all comes undone.

Here too, engaging in potentially hard conversations (particularly in multinational or multicultural contexts) requires diligence. It is all too common to find out that even the written words on a contract are understood differently by others. Fortunately there are several excellent resources and seminars available specifically on how to engage with difficult discussions. Researching the options and trainers accessible in your region and budget requires only a few minutes but offers a resource that may have dramatic benefit.

It is better to risk offence by striving for clarity than to stumble into problems by assumption; assumptions are the seeds of future conflict.

Part of my role with Catalyst Foundation has involved offering grants to various charities. Early on, we committed funds to an organization whose leaders were two men I have known and appreciated for a number of years. When they reported on the project we had agreed to fund, I was surprised to learn that they had decided to send only one staff member for the supported training rather than the two that had been proposed, without telling us why. I was annoyed.

Catalyst has always preferred an informal approach to philanthropy, but in that case it contributed to a situation that required some tough conversations and strained relationships. Eventually we worked it all out, but I learned a lesson about Clarity.

Since then, I've learned to be much more intentional and explicit about expectations, including a process for communicating changes in the initial plan.

If all of this seems like a lot of work that will slow down important work, you're right. Clarity is a demanding element of healthy culture. It takes time, energy, resources, and discipline that can feel like a drag to some of us.

Not only that, but it is an ongoing issue. You can't achieve clarity now and expect it to remain solid for years, or even weeks to come. It must become a continuous matter of attention and intention to resist the natural tendency for things to degrade over time.

But doing the hard work at the beginning and building regular practices of both formal updates and immediate expectation checks can maintain the kind of clarity that make unnecessary duplication of effort and costly gaps in the system far less frequent and damaging.

And clarity is a system, or more accurately a system of systems that empower every person, department, and partner to give their best efforts in the ways that bring the best results for the entire organization. It's worth the work.

# The Elements – Trust

"The best way to find out if you can trust somebody is to trust them." – Ernest Hemingway

"Trust is the glue of life. It's the most essential ingredient in effective communication. It's the foundational principle that holds all relationships."
– Stephen Covey

Trust is the last of the elements of culture listed on the REACTION Dashboard, but it is definitely not the least. In fact, it serves as the crucial foundation that determines the potential of all the rest. Trust is the predominant relational aspect of every culture. Without it, nothing else can work; and with it, a lot of potentially problematic gaps can be overcome.

We can almost all, sadly, relate to the experience of working with someone we couldn't trust. It is always frustrating, if not miserable. A lack of trust is the surest drain on our enthusiasm and ultimately of our effectiveness. We simply can't give our best in an environment where we don't have trust.

As obvious as this may seem, there is some complexity involved. Not every failure of trust is the same. And there are several factors that contribute to the ease or difficulty of building and maintaining trust.

At a basic level, trust refers to at least two components: character and competence. In practice it is the combination of these two that determines the appropriate level of trust.

**Trust is a combination of character and competence.**

1. **Competence**: The knowledge and ability necessary to accomplish the expectations.

Several years ago I was part of a group doing a high ropes course activity at a retreat. The camp staff who were responsible for us ensured that everyone was properly harnessed and tied in to the safety rope before letting us climb sixty feet in the air to attempt a variety of challenging physical tasks on beams, cables, and logs. I'd spent much of the preceding five years leading similar activities and had trained hundreds of people in safe techniques.

As some of my friends worked their way up and across the obstacles, I noticed that the camp staff seemed to be making a fairly basic mistake in how they were handling the ropes. It was a small error but it could have been devastating if a fall happened at the wrong instant. I try to avoid correcting other leaders in public but, in this case of real danger, I had to say something. I approached the leader of the team and told him I was concerned about what I was seeing, and that I thought they were doing something unsafe.

Thankfully, the response was sincere, appreciative, and apologetic. He told me they hadn't overseen this activity in some time and had simply forgotten the proper technique. He immediately alerted the other staff and they all corrected what they were doing.

The danger they caused was a matter of competence. They hadn't refreshed their skills often enough and they were doing it wrong. I couldn't trust them to keep any of us safe until they became competent again.

The same scenario happens in every industry. People are put in positions or given responsibilities that they aren't equipped for effectively. It may be their fault—if they pretend they know how to do something they really don't—or it may be a matter of insufficient training or supervision, as it was at the camp. Wherever the fault lies, a lack of competence is a risk and we should not trust someone who isn't able to do the job.

Fortunately, in many cases the solution for lacking competence is education, training, coaching and/or supervision. Technical skills can often be acquired, at least to an acceptable standard, providing there is sufficient will and investment.

Of course there are exceptions. Some qualifications and abilities are prerequisites for a variety of legal, liability, or performance reasons. These are usually identifiable from the beginning of the hiring process. Less frequently, growth or change requires increased competence from a team member who is just not up to the task. Restructuring the role or transitioning the person may be necessary if they aren't able to reach the required ability.

2. **Character**: The moral and ethical will to fulfill commitments.

I could say that I've been spoiled because I have never been in an employment situation where my boss asked me to violate my integrity or where their behaviour demonstrated that they were fundamentally corrupt. I wish that were the case for everyone, but it isn't.

The continuous news cycle of scandal and falls from grace reveals on a daily basis that character is an issue in every industry, and from the grassroots to the highest levels of leadership. It is all too easy to become jaded and cynical in light of so many public failures, let alone the more private ones we may experience in our own circumstances.

And the most honest among us might have the courage and humility to admit that we don't entirely live up to our own high standards.

Trusting someone's character means that we don't have to second-guess their motives or commitment. We can believe that they will dedicate themselves to accomplishing what they've agreed to accomplish. And that they will do so in a way that honours the values we share.

To simplify: *Trust is the belief that people will do their best (Character) and that their best will be good enough (Competence).*

Individual Trust

When using the REACTION Dashboard, the Individual Trust space is scored according to how well you trust your Organization. As much as we'd like to believe that would come easily, it's actually often a dynamic rating. Several factors come into play.

First, each Individual has a particular default setting for Trust. The family, cultural, and experiential influences that shape these preferences are complex. Some of us tend to trust easily, even to a fault, while others are generally more suspicious. Neither is necessarily preferable.

People who have experienced significant letdowns or betrayals can understandably find it difficult to trust others, and this can serve them well in many situations. Those who assume the Roy Rogers' maxim that "A stranger is just a friend you haven't met yet" and extend trust easily often have a head-start at the beginning of relationships, but they can be vulnerable to naiveté and feelings of great betrayal if the trust is misplaced or not reciprocated.

An awareness of our basic tendency to trust quickly or slowly can be a useful way to moderate the downsides of our inclination. All of us experience situations that increase and decrease our level of trust in our organization.

Trust is fragile. How much trust we feel at any particular time can vary significantly. One harsh email or passive/aggressive comment can reduce our trust instantly, and it can take days to recover, if we recover at all. Wise leaders pay close attention to what triggers our suspicions or feelings of betrayal, looking for factors that may provoke an out-of-scale response that may not be entirely warranted.

It is dangerous for any leader when they feel low trust for their organization for any extended period of time. If it can't be remedied, there is no healthy option except for the leader to leave and find a new environment where trust can be established. There can be no lasting leadership without mutual trust.

<u>Organizational Trust</u>

Trust is relational, so in an organization, trust represents the connections between every individual and each other person. It is a complex web of relationships. Managing the sheer volume of interpersonal dynamics can seem overwhelming to even the most committed leader.

Fortunately there are some fairly simple things that we can do to help increase the level of Trust in any organization without getting lost in the potential drama and distraction that may occur. It definitely takes work, but the benefits to the culture and to the bottom line are worth it.

First, we need to treat team members as adults. There needs to be an understanding that each individual is responsible for their own behaviour and will be held accountable for it. Communicating values clearly and consistently from the very beginning of the employment process sets a strong tone. Then we must follow up by modelling adherence to those values and welcoming correction when we cross a line.

When Jesus saw people pretending to hold positive values but not living them out on a daily basis, he challenged them using the local word for theatre actors: hypocrites. There are few accusations that damage trust more deeply than being a hypocrite.

Of course, none of us are perfect. It is often the way we respond to our own transgressions that has the biggest impact on trust. Those who minimize or attempt to justify their own errors validate the hypocrite label and further undermine their credibility. It doesn't take long for even highly productive leaders to lose all their influence when they develop a pattern of ignoring their own failures while holding others accountable.

In contrast, it is amazing how much trust can be built by a sincere apology.

A humble acknowledgment of our mistakes, asking for help in areas of inexperience or weakness, and admitting the ways we have hurt or frustrated others is a far too rare habit for some leaders. The desire to present ourselves as exemplary too often becomes an insecure need to appear perfect. No one believes it and it makes us look foolish or desperate.

Little acts of honesty and kindness build trust. When leaders go first with some basic vulnerability, it creates a safe space for others to do the same. Like a piggy bank, the deposits are usually small, but the withdrawals are bigger. We need to be intentional about accumulating trust for the inevitable times when we will need to draw on it to advance a project, gain support, or deal with problems.

Some leaders demand loyalty. They place a high value on it in a way that makes unflinching allegiance the standard. This is not Trust; it is a dangerous manipulation that denies the very nature of human relationships. Real Trust is earned, never imposed or required. Subservience and acquiescence are not trust; they are responses to authority run amok. Meaningful commitment is an ongoing process that relies on mutual service, humility, and respect. It is never coerced.

In a healthy organization, Trust shows up in the willingness people have to support one another and give one another the benefit of the doubt. There is an efficiency of relationship that allows for both more focus on what matters most and a casual familiarity. Capable people who actually enjoy being together are more likely to go above and beyond when the need arises. All of this improves results over time.

Network Trust

Contracts are one expression of trust. They establish the parameters of the interactions between two or more parties for their mutual satisfaction. But this is an incomplete form.

Trust is much more the feeling stakeholders experience when they think of your organization than the details of your agreements. It is more about your reputation than your ability to craft a memorandum of understanding.

Network Trust is essentially the belief your diverse connections have that you will fulfill your commitments to them, and your confidence that they will do the same. No matter how big your organization or network, this comes down to human relationships. Every positive interaction makes your brand more trustworthy and every poor one undermines it.

This is more than public relations and media training. It is the sum of the way every one of your people deals with everyone outside your team. You can't spin it or fake it for long.

Examples of large corporations that have lost the public trust are so common these days, it is an embarrassment. It seems there is no industry that can maintain integrity consistently and far too many mismanage their mistakes, compounding the damage. Ultimately the result is that we all become more skeptical, or even cynical, of everything.

Recognizing this growing reality offers an underlying opportunity for those leaders and organizations that are willing to make a greater commitment to following their values and being transparent. Our society is increasingly hungry for things that we can believe in. Trustworthiness is becoming a competitive advantage, which may be a sad statement but is something that leaders can leverage for greater impact if we can live up to the challenge of being trustworthy.

That challenge requires leaders to pay attention to both people and tasks. Trust is not a group of happy people who really like each other but get nothing done, nor is it driven performers who are prepared to avoid being stabbed in the back by their colleagues. Trust is a commitment to doing the little relational things that grow into big things, and to continuous improvement of skills and systems. It's not fluffy at all.

Trust is the bedrock that makes lasting impact possible.

# The Elements – Celebration

"The more you praise and celebrate your life, the more there is in life to celebrate" – Oprah Winfrey
"Until further notice – Celebrate everything!" – Anonymous

I have become convinced that Celebration is one of the most powerful and least used tools available for leaders to get better results.

Many leaders assume celebration is soft, even childish. Their minds immediately go to cupcakes and balloons in the break room on someone's birthday, or silly rah-rah activities that have no relationship to the real work of the organization. Those concerns are valid. The kind of celebration we want is intimately connected to the success of our organization and the results we achieve. Cupcakes and balloons are fun, and they may make the office a happier place, but we want more.

Celebration that makes a legitimate difference in culture has to be relevant.

We really want something that is related to real results. Otherwise the fun feels somewhat empty and the prizes are quickly discarded or forgotten.

Human beings are innately wired for celebration. It connects us not only to one another, but to the part of ourselves that wants to succeed. Every culture has rituals of celebration, from the most ancient to today. People have festivals and events; we sing, dance, and laugh when we achieve success. And the greater the success, the more powerful the celebration. We are made to party.

Politics, sports, the arts, and business have their own ways of recognizing success and outstanding performances. We give awards, we offer incentives, we intuitively tap into our capacity for celebration in ways that are almost religious. And in many ways that is what they are.

The Old Testament (Jewish Scriptures) gives many examples of both spontaneous celebrations (i.e., David dancing passionately as the ark of the covenant is returned to Jerusalem) and highly structured ones (i.e., the elaborate instructions for offering sacrifices throughout the book of Leviticus). Every religion has its own examples of celebrations meant to remind us of the most important truths and events of our spiritual tradition.

And it's not just religious communities. The Olympics provide us with excellent examples of celebration of many kinds. We can learn from these examples of Individual, Organization, and Network celebrations.

Individual Celebration

When an athlete crosses the finish line and pumps their fist or lets out a triumphant yell, they are demonstrating the most elemental form of celebration. Having devoted their lives to their sport for years and made massive effort and sacrifice, they can't help but let out a spontaneous outburst of elation from accomplishing something difficult and meaningful.

Shortly afterwards, the top three performers are invited to stand on the podium, receive gold, silver, and bronze medals, and see the flag of the champion's country raised while their national anthem is played. This well staged ritual of Celebration is so familiar that we rarely question why there are three medals (not 2 or 5) and why those materials have come to so strongly represent first, second, and third place. We accept the significance of this established celebration and honour those who achieve it.

As individuals we can engage in both spontaneous and planned celebrations. Most of us do this naturally, but not as often or as well as we could. Adding intention to celebration can provide us with greater motivations, and can help ensure we don't miss the opportunity to pause and take note of what has enabled our success. Celebration breaks up the rushed rhythm of life and causes us to actually recognize our achievements.

Leaders often struggle to celebrate as individuals. While it is admirable to have a strong team focus, it is also important to find appropriate ways to personally celebrate the accomplishments to which we ourselves have significantly contributed. Additionally, since leaders are often "on duty" at team and organizational celebrations they may not feel free to participate fully.

Identifying specific and satisfying ways to celebrate achievements enables leaders to tap into a deeper level of their own motivation, just as it does for followers. Don't let the anticipation of the next challenge or the reality that not everything is complete rob you of the benefits of celebrating progress and the steps along the way to perfection. This isn't tolerating mediocrity or wasting time; it is refuelling our tank for the next part of the road.

A *note on introverts*: At every summer camp I ever worked at, campers who had their birthday during camp had to do some variation of standing on their chair, skipping around the dining hall, or being thrown in the lake, while the whole camp sang and cheered. For some campers this was the absolute highlight of the summer, but for others, the intensity of being the centre of attention was overwhelming and upsetting. What was intended as a joyful moment became quite the opposite. The tradition didn't factor in the needs and preferences of the very person we were celebrating.

Celebrations don't need to be elaborate, public extravaganzas. Simple and personal recognitions can be just as powerful if they fit the personalities and preferences of those we want to celebrate. A quiet stop at the ice cream shop or time spent writing and reflecting on a proud moment may be deeply significant.

I do encourage even strongly inclined introverts to include at least one other trusted person in their celebrations. This is partly to increase the likelihood that they happen at all, and partly to add some external energy and affirmation to help the celebration be more authentic and meaningful.

Organizational Celebration

Watch teammates cheer as one of their own approaches a finish line and you get a sense of what celebration can mean in an organization. The joy, tears, yelling, hugging, and clapping demonstrates that humans are wired to celebrate together.

Identifying ways to celebrate small and large accomplishments in ways that inspire continued effort and greater focus on the things that bring results is a sadly underdeveloped skill in many organizations. This means those who commit to doing it well can quickly have a significant competitive advantage. The challenge is primarily one of will and awareness.

Committed leaders take time to understand what their team values, both in their efforts and in recognition.

It is also important to carefully consider which accomplishments are worthy of celebration. In most organizations this list is much too short. Healthy organizations look for opportunities to celebrate not only completed success, but the more frequent examples of relevant progress. They take advantage of chances to reinforce what matters most and to demonstrate that the team is "winning" in as many ways as possible.

Of course this must be sincere. Pandering to underachievers, denying reality, or pretending everything is wonderful when it obviously isn't only leads to disillusionment and loss of leadership credibility. But most leaders err on the side of insufficient celebration, not too much.

Ask yourself:

- What are the behaviours you want to encourage?
- What benchmarks show you're on the right track?
- What is the earliest evidence of significant success?

These are all opportunities for celebration.

While leaders are typically motivated by completing projects, many people benefit from celebrating the interim steps along the way. And celebration needs to prioritize those being celebrated.

This means that both the cause for celebration and the form of celebration are focused on the preferences of the people, not those of the leader. Leaders often have less need for, and less appreciation of, Celebration than anyone else in their Organization. Stretching in this area is a smart move for leaders who want to multiply their impact.

**Leaders often have less need for and less appreciation of Celebration than anyone else in their Organization.**

Common examples of celebration include team parties and dinners, bonuses, paid vacations, and extra time off. All of those may have a place, but there are more creative possibilities.

One charity I know worked in remote offices. During their conference calls they developed a form of celebration I love: when anyone secured a particularly large donation, the entire team would stand on their chairs, each in their own workspaces across the country, and clap and cheer. It was initially spontaneous, a little silly, and potentially even embarrassing, but it quickly became a kind of rallying point for the team and something they anticipated eagerly.

A youth hockey program I convened decided that instead of giving a Player of the Game award, we would have a special jersey made up for the player who demonstrated hustle, teamwork, and sportsmanship. For it to be meaningful, we knew it couldn't just be given to each player in turn, but to someone who had truly shown those key qualities.

Your team may be able to organically generate celebrations that can become unique and meaningful rituals. Pay attention to how good news is shared and responded to. It is a solid clue about how people prefer to celebrate.

Too many leaders shut down celebrations, either intentionally or just because their persona in the office sends the message that they are not interested. Organizations typically resemble their leader; leaders who don't celebrate create the expectation that doing so is a waste of time and resources. When the boss joins in on the celebration, it validates the impulse from the team and deepens connections.

The truth is, even though leaders may have a harder time embracing celebration, those who do are healthier, happier, and more influential within their organization than those who resist it. They attract and retain highly motivated people who get results because every time results are celebrated, it reinforces the possibility and importance of success. Leaders who celebrate get more out of employees, donors and volunteers because the organization is optimistic, productive, and even fun.

Celebration doesn't just follow success; it helps make it happen.

Network Celebration

We've all seen fans go wild when their team wins, even though the fans did nothing more than watch from their seats or couches. We long to be part of success. We want to associate ourselves with excellence. It inspires us.

It also shows that our need for celebration isn't being fully met in our own lives. We need more, and we want to share it with others.

To use the language of REACTION, our networks may have a different Reason than we do, their Energy may be hard to access, keeping Alignment with them may be an ongoing struggle to maintain Clarity, and there may be any number of factors straining Trust—but if you can find ways to sincerely Celebrate with them you will find all the hurdles get a little smaller.

Charities understand the need to celebrate with their donors. The best of them send reports, share stories and statistics, offer personal thank yous, and hold events where they acknowledge the ways donors have made impact possible. But then, charities have little choice—without committed donors they'd cease to exist.

Is there really a place in the hard-nosed world of business for celebrating with our networks?

There is for leaders who want to get the best possible results.

Regardless of the sector, celebrating with your network strengthens bonds, reinforces the benefits of relationship, and ignites greater interest. The challenge is doing it in a way that breaks through the constant noise of contemporary life.

# User's Guide to The REACTION Dashboard

Leaders have used the REACTION Dashboard to understand, assess, and improve the culture of their organizations for several years. In that time, the tool has been continually adjusted and improved. It has been tested in contexts I'd never imagined, and has consistently been found helpful. All of that exploration of the tool has shown some clear patterns of how to get the most value out of it.

Here's a step by step practical guide to using the REACTION Dashboard in your context.

1. The Dashboard

A copy of the REACTION Dashboard worksheet is at the end of this chapter. But it is equally good to just grab a scrap of paper and draw your own. One of the valuable aspects of the tool is that it is so so simple to use. Write the word REACT vertically on your page (or journal, or napkin, or tablet, or whatever). Then add IONS above for the columns and you're ready to go.

Fill in Reason, Energy, Alignment, Clarity, and Trust for the rows and Individual, Organization, Network, and Special for the Columns.

|  | Individual | Organization | Network | Special |
|---|---|---|---|---|
| Reason |  |  |  |  |
| Energy |  |  |  |  |
| Alignment |  |  |  |  |
| Clarity |  |  |  |  |
| Trust |  |  |  |  |

2. Scoring

A 1-10 point system has become the default approach to scoring the elements of culture, with 10 representing a situation where things could not possibly get better, and 1 being the absolute worst-case scenario. You can substitute letter grades, stoplight colours, or emojis if you prefer. What matters is not the scores you ascribe, but the situations they represent.

|           | Individual | Organization | Network | Special |
|-----------|------------|--------------|---------|---------|
| Reason    | 9          | 8            | 7       | 8       |
| Energy    | 7          | 6            | 8       | 8       |
| Alignment | 9          | 9            | 9       | 9       |
| Clarity   | 6          | 8            | 7       | 6       |
| Trust     | 9          | 8            | 8       | 9       |

Remember that this is a Dashboard. It works best when the scores reflect the current state of things, not the average of the last quarter, year, or season. Like the displays on your car, immediate information is the purpose. Trends and patterns will reveal themselves when you identify Warning Lights and Celebrations.

If you need a reminder of the meaning of any of the REACT Elements, flip back to the Elements chapters. They give greater content to describe each element, and offer lots of tips for addressing Warning Lights and Celebrations

Scoring shouldn't take long. Don't get stuck debating between two numbers. Pick one, use a decimal if you have to, or write both options in. In the end the scores don't matter; it's the realities and perceptions they represent that will determine your next leadership actions.

When using REACTION with a group, remind them that

comparing numbers is not helpful. They are subjective opinions, not definitive statistics. Today's score of 6 for me could be a 7 tomorrow, and it may be a 5 for you. There are too many factors informing how high or low we tend to score elements to begin listing them here. What matters is the reason for the numbers. And that's what Warning Lights begin to expose.

3. <u>Warning Lights</u>

Warning Lights are indicators of danger, whether immediate or approaching. Identify two scores on your chart that relate to situations that have the potential to have a negative impact on your organization. Typically, these are marked by drawing a triangle (a common symbol of danger) around the number.

|  | Individual | Organization | Network | Special |
|---|---|---|---|---|
| Reason | 9 | 8 | 7 | 8 |
| Energy | 7 | ⚠6 | 8 | 8 |
| Alignment | 9 | 9 | 9 | 9 |
| Clarity | 6 | 8 | ⚠7 | 6 |
| Trust | 9 | 8 | 8 | 9 |

It's important to remember that these may not be the lowest scores. They can be, but they may equally be scores that are trending in the wrong direction, or are just relevant to areas of great importance in the current season for your work. If you have a hard time choosing between possibilities, consider which option has the greatest impact on the organization at this point and in the months to come.

Some have asked why specifically two Warning Lights. This is a judgment call based on experience. Identifying more makes it hard to focus on how to improve things; choosing fewer may mean ignoring something important. Ultimately, if anyone insists on more or less than two Warning Lights, it is not worth debating. What matters is that they are able to take action to address them.

After identifying the Warning Lights we ask three questions to begin the problem solving process.

1. Whose problem is this?

The point of this question is to identify the right people to be involved in finding a way to address the issue. It is rare, but possible, that there may be a Warning Light that an individual can properly handle alone. In the vast majority of cases it will take a small group to sort things out.

Some leaders are tempted to make the circle too large. They want to include everyone in solving the problem, perhaps to draw on the wisdom of the whole team. This is usually a mistake. It is better to seriously consider who needs to be involved. The rule of thumb for problem solving is to include everyone who needs to be included and no one who doesn't.

2. What needs to be done to address the issue?

This is not the same thing as having a complete plan to solve the problem. If we already know exactly how to solve it, we should already be doing so. That would be like pulling into the gas station just as the low fuel light comes on. All that's required is to follow through.

More frequently, leaders know some of the aspects involved in addressing the Warning Light but not everything. This question invites them to list what they can identify at this point as a way of clarifying the situation. It may reveal a complete process, but it may only show the trailhead that will lead the way.

3. What can you do today to start the process?

In practice, the specific timing involved in this question is flexible. I often give leaders until the end of the next day to take the first step.

What's critical is that they commit to doing something very soon. It may be as simple as sending a message to some of the people they believe need to be involved in solving the problem, asking for a meeting. It may be blocking off time on their calendar a couple weeks out to devote their attention to the issue. It involves taking initiative to get the ball rolling.

Too often we identify a risk and put off doing something until we know everything we need to do. That is self-defeating. Warning Lights rarely improve when we ignore them. Taking the first step is often enough to ensure that a resolution will be found.

One of the benefits of the REACTION Dashboard is that Warning Lights reveal problems early. Seeing them sooner means they are more manageable and that we have a chance to address them before they grow. Since most leaders thrive on solving problems, identifying them and taking initial action is a solid start to avoiding the danger and damage they reveal.

4. <u>Celebrations</u>

This is often the hard part of the process for many leaders. We tend to undervalue Celebration and give it less attention and energy than it deserves because we are absorbed in solving problems and doing all the other things leadership requires.

However, time spent identifying and acting on those elements of the REACTION Dashboard that indicate some evidence of positive impact or progress is one of the most beneficial aspects of the process. (See the chapter "The Elements: Celebration" for more on the leverageable advantage of Celebration).

As with Warning Lights, leaders choose two Celebrations from among the elements. Drawing a circle around their score is one way to distinguish them from Warning Lights, but some prefer a more evocative symbol like a party hat or a star.

|           | Individual | Organization | Network | Special |
|-----------|------------|--------------|---------|---------|
| Reason    | (9)        | 8            | 7       | 8       |
| Energy    | 7          | /6\          | 8       | 8       |
| Alignment | 9          | (9)          | 9       | 9       |
| Clarity   | 6          | 8            | /7\     | 6       |
| Trust     | 9          | 8            | 8       | 9       |

Once again, Celebrations may be the highest scores on the worksheet, but not always. A lower score that is improving or one that is holding strong against strong negative influence may be the best thing currently happening.

It is important to remember that Celebrations are tied to what is truly meaningful to the organization. Some leaders resist Celebration as light, soft, or silly. That misconception costs them a valuable way to impact people. Taking every opportunity to reinforce what is important, what is working, and that progress and success are possible is something that separates the healthiest leaders and organizations from those that never approach their potential.

The three questions for Celebrations are similar to those for Warning Lights, but with some significant differences.

1. Who can be included in the Celebration?

Celebrations are most impactful when they are leveraged to impact more people. Contrary to Warning Lights and problem solving, we want the circle as large as we can justify for Celebrations. This invites everyone to share the good news, and reminds them all of what we are striving for and what is going well.

Logistics and situations may limit the ability to include the most people in any particular Celebration, but finding ways to spread the good news as widely through the Organization (and in many cases the Network as well) is a best practice.

2. How can we Celebrate in a way that is meaningful for those we want to recognize?

This is the pitfall of Celebration. When we don't consider what will be appreciated and appropriate by the people most responsible for what we are celebrating, we can undermine our attempts and unintentionally send the wrong message. Some leaders need to deliberately take the time to understand their people to discover what matters to them.

Celebrations don't have to be expensive in resources, time, or effort; but they must be seen as sincere. This means that leaders can't skip them, appear half-hearted, or always delegate Celebration to others. Leaders set the tone in this area and must demonstrate their belief that Celebration is important and worthwhile.

3. What can you do today to ensure this isn't missed?

When we ignore Warning Lights they tend to get worse until they demand our attention. Celebrations that are ignored appear to simply disappear, but over time they drain the organization of energy and engagement. It is an opportunity cost, and one that happens far too often.

For this reason, I encourage leaders to take the first step to ensure that doesn't happen. Sending a note of appreciation, scheduling a lunch or meeting, ordering flowers, or setting a time to figure out how to celebrate well takes only a few moments, but it is a strategic priority for leaders who want to build a culture of Celebration that leads to health, engagement, and excellent results.

**Frequently Asked Questions**

*Should we take time during a REACTION Dashboard group session to process Warning Lights and Celebrations together?*

Probably. When time allows, it is helpful to provide an opportunity for people to raise any Warning Lights they've identified if the people in the room are the right ones to be involved in solving the problem. It's a great way to take immediate action. The exceptions would be when this is misused to publicly complain or attack a colleague, or to abdicate responsibility for addressing the Warning Lights by passing them off to others.

Sharing Celebrations together is a powerful way to encourage the group and to reinforce the best of what you do together. Be aware that this should be only he first step in making Celebration a vibrant part of the organization's culture. Going beyond a brief acknowledgment of positive impact is needed to make it really stick.

*How often should we do the REACTION Dashboard?*

Once you are familiar with the tool, it takes only a few minutes to complete the entire four-step process and identify your four action steps (two for Warning Lights and two for Celebrations). There is no financial cost and it can be done anywhere. It can be done as an individual, with a core team, or even with an entire organization. I've even facilitated sessions where several stakeholders from the network were involved.

That flexibility means the REACTION Dashboard can be used as often as you find it useful. Some leaders have a routine of doing a REACTION session with their team quarterly. Some do it on their own monthly. There is no definitive rhythm that is best.

At minimum, using the tool with a leadership team or board of directors annually gives immediate insights into the organization that might otherwise be missed. After a few cycles, it becomes an intuitive part of how you approach your leadership.

It can also be very effective to have the REACTION Dashboard in your back pocket for any time when it seems your culture is struggling. Having a quick and effective way to explore where things may be stuck can guide the conversation to greater insight with less confusion or conflict.

*Do we need an outside facilitator to get the most out of the REACTION Dashboard?*

Generally no. The tool is simple enough that it can be managed quite well internally. However, having a skilled and experienced facilitator guide you through the REACTION Dashboard initially may add emphasis and utility you won't discover on your own.

Consider using an outside facilitator if it is likely that the leader may be a significant factor in some Warning Lights. Credibility and openness are increased if there is minimal appearance of bias. An effective facilitator will support leaders, but not protect them from criticism or accountability. If things get tense, the steadiness of an outside voice may enable greater progress.

As with any leadership development, the payoff comes from application. Outside facilitators can bring you and your team to the point of defining your action steps, but you still have to take them. Peer accountability is the most reliable way to get results.

*Are there other applications for the REACTION Dashboard?*

I've been surprised at some of the ways leaders have made use of the tool to understand, assess, and improve their leadership and their organizational culture. It has been used to mediate conflict, as part of a performance review, for board development, and during strategic planning. If you find another way that the REACTION Dashboard helps develop healthy leaders and healthy organizations I'd love to hear about it.

# The REACTION Dashboard Worksheet

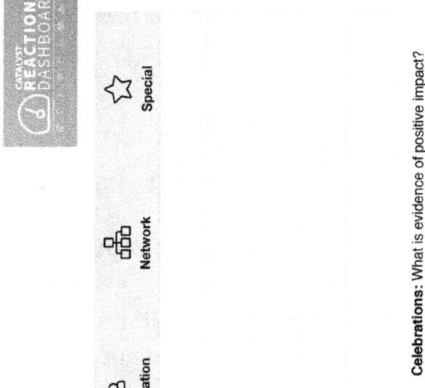

**Elements of Healthy Culture**
- Reason
- Energy
- Alignment
- Clarity
- Trust

Individual · Organization · Network · Special

**Warning Lights:** What indicates danger?

Who needs to be part of the solution?

What needs to be done to address this issue in a timely manner?

What steps am I taking in the next 36 hours to get started?

**Celebrations:** What is evidence of positive impact?

Who can be part of the celebration?

What should be done to ensure this is addressed in a way that is meaningful to those being celebrated?

What steps am I taking in the next 36 hours to ensure this isn't missed?

*Chris Wignall, Catalyst Foundation www.catalystfoundation.ca*

# A Final Word

I am completely convinced of the power of leadership. Done well it brings enormous good to the world. Done poorly, exactly the opposite occurs. More and more, the difference between doing leadership well and doing it poorly is found not in strategy or execution but in culture.

> **The difference between doing leadership well and doing it poorly is found not in strategy or execution but in culture.**

There are all kinds of reasons why leaders don't effectively address issues of culture. It's hard. It's fuzzy. It's outside of our training. And it doesn't seem to have obvious direct impact on the bottom line. With all the urgent and important demands on the time and energy of leadership it can be understandable for culture to be overlooked.

If you've read this far you know better. You have at least a sense that there is more to leading than strategy and execution. You want your work to be both impactful and enjoyable. You get that the people you lead want and deserve something more. And you're willing to do the hard stuff that makes the great stuff happen.

But it may not be intuitive for you. That's why I wrote this book.

The REACTION Dashboard is one of the simplest tools on your leadership utility belt. It's also a very useful one. It can help you to make leading culture practical, clear, and actionable. It gives you something you need to be the kind of leader you would gladly follow. The kind of leader who gets great results while maintaining a context where people can thrive. The kind of leader who lasts and leaves a legacy they can be proud of. The kind of leader you want to be.

My prayer in offering this book is that you will excel in leadership that is good, lasting, and significant, wherever you may lead. We all need a lot more of that.

If I can be helpful in your leadership or you have any insights about The REACTION Dashboard please contact me: chris@catalystfoundation.ca

www.reactiondashboard.com

# About The Author

Chris Wignall is fascinated by how people and organizations work (or don't). As the Executive Director of Catalyst Foundation (www.catalystfoundation.ca) he comes alongside charity leaders to help them lead more effectively and enhance the impact of their organizations. Past work as a pastor, church planter, camp director, corporate trainer, whitewater kayak instructor, and clown all inform his approach. Chris lives beside a beautiful waterfall in Greensville, Ontario with his wife and three children, spending as much time running, paddling, and exploring as they can; and he rarely turns down Coke, chicken wings, or chocolate fudge.

www.ingramcontent.com/pod-product-compliance
Lightning Source LLC
Chambersburg PA
CBHW070149080526
44586CB00015B/1913